Series / Number 07-064

D0768386

LATENT
CLASS
ANALYSIS

ALLAN L. McCUTCHEON
University of Delaware

SAGE PUBLICATIONS
The International Professional Publishers
Newbury Park   London   New Delhi

For information address:

 SAGE Publications, Inc.
2455 Teller Road
Newbury Park, California 91320
E-mail: order@sagepub.com

SAGE Publications Ltd.
6 Bonhill Street
London EC2A 4PU
United Kingdom

SAGE Publications India Pvt. Ltd.
M-32 Market
Greater Kailash I
New Delhi 110 048 India

Printed in the United States of America

International Standard Book Number 0-8039-2752-5

Library of Congress Catalog Card No. L.C. 87-061277

96 97 98 99 00 01 02 12 11 10 9 8 7 6

When citing a professional paper, please use the proper form. Remember to cite the correct Sage University Paper series title and include the paper number. One of the two following formats can be adapted (depending on the style manual used):

(1) McCutcheon, A. L. (1987). *Latent class analysis* (Sage University Paper series on Quantitative Applications in the Social Sciences, No. 07-064). Newbury Park, CA: Sage.

OR

(2) McCutcheon, A. L. 1987. *Latent class analysis*. Sage University Paper series on Quantitative Applications in the Social Sciences, series no. 07-064. Newbury Park, CA: Sage.

ACKNOWLEDGMENTS

The author gratefully acknowledges the helpful comments of Lisa Crockett, William Eaton, Kenneth Eckhardt, Valerie Hans, and two anonymous reviewers on earlier drafts of this paper.

The data utilized in this book were made available in part by the Inter-university Consortium for Political and Social Research. The data were originally collected by the Center for Political Studies at the University of Michigan. Neither the original source or collecters of the data nor the Consortium bear any responsibility for the analyses or interpretations presented here.

CONTENTS

Series Editor's Introduction   4

1. **Introduction: The Logic of Latent Variables**   5

   Basic Orientation   5
   What Is Latent Class Analysis?   7
   General Outline of Presentation   10

2. **Latent Class Analysis**   11

   Local Independence   14
   The Formal Latent Class Model   17
   Maximum Likelihood Estimation   21

3. **Estimating Latent Categorical Variables**   27

   Exploratory Latent Class Analyses   28
   Confirmatory Latent Class Analysis   37

4. **Analyzing Scale Response Patterns**   44

   Models with Errors of Measurement   49
   Goodman's Scale Model   56

5. **Comparing Latent Structures Among Groups**   61

   Simultaneous Latent Structure Model   62
   Heterogeneous T-Class Model   68
   Homogeneity Models   71

6. **Conclusions**   79

Appendix A   81

Appendix B   89

References   93

About the Author   96

Series Editor's Introduction

In Latent Class Analysis, Allan L. McCutcheon introduces readers to a rapidly developing methodology for analyzing categorical data. Latent class analysis enables a characterization of categorical latent (unobserved) variables from an analysis of the structure of the relationships among several categorical manifest (observed) variables. The method, which is often referred to as a "categorical data analogue to factor analysis," was originally conceived of as an analytic method for survey data. As an exploratory technique, latent class analysis can be used to reduce a set of several categorically scored variables into a single latent variable with a set of underlying types or "classes." As a confirmatory method, the latent class model can be used to test hypotheses regarding the researcher's a priori assertions about the structure of the relationships among the observed variables. Recent developments in latent class technology hold great promise for making this methodology one of the most powerful and flexible modeling techniques for survey researchers and others who wish to examine the structure of the relationships among two or more categorically scored variables.

Professor McCutcheon emphasizes the rationale for using latent class analysis, discussing the logic and application of the formal latent class model in the earlier chapters. Exploratory and confirmatory applications of the latent class model are also discussed and illustrated in these first chapters. Chapter 4 covers the use of the latent class model for examining the scaling properties of a set of survey items. There is an extended example of American electoral participation that builds on the logic of Guttman scaling and examines the later extensions of the scale analysis proposed by Proctor, Lazarsfeld, Goodman, and others. Chapter 5 is devoted to an important new development in latent class analysis—the ability to model simultaneously the latent structure of two or more populations. This application of the method provides survey analysts with a powerful new method for comparative analysis.

As with most of the volumes in this series, anyone with a good practical knowledge of algebra should have little difficulty reading this monograph. Survey analysts and researchers from most social science disciplines should find this introduction to the topic relevant and easy to read.

—*Richard G. Niemi*
Series Co-Editor

LATENT CLASS ANALYSIS

ALLAN L. MCCUTCHEON
University of Delaware

1. INTRODUCTION: THE LOGIC OF LATENT VARIABLES

BASIC ORIENTATION

Many concepts in the social sciences cannot be observed directly. We cannot, for example, directly observe authoritarianism, economic development, racial prejudice, alienation, anomie, or religious commitment. Indeed, there are hundreds of other theoretically interesting concepts for which the available measures are assumed to be imperfect indicators. For example, while we cannot directly observe religious commitment, we are likely to believe that a high level of commitment leads people to attend church more frequently, pray more frequently, conduct themselves with greater behavioral orthodoxy, report that their religious beliefs are of great importance to them, and so forth. Because we believe that each of the observed indicators is caused by an unobserved, or *latent*, variable of interest, we expect covariation among the observed measures, and we study the patterns of interrelationships among the observed indicators to understand and characterize the underlying latent variable. A number of recent methodological advances enable researchers to systematically analyze these relationships, thus permitting better characterization of the latent variables of interest.

The basic premise of the study of latent variables is that the covariation actually observed among the manifest (observed) variables is due to each manifest variable's relationship to the latent variable—that the latent variable "explains" the relationships between the observed variables. If such a variable exists, and can be characterized, then controlling for this latent variable will result in diminishing the covariation between all of the observed variables to the level of chance covariation. Consequently, the latent variable is said to be the "true" source of the originally observed covariations. For example, we are likely to characterize a latent variable as religious commitment if, within the limits of chance covariation, it explains the relationships observed among measures for frequency of church attendance, frequency of prayer, and self-reported importance of religion.

Much of the early work on the study of latent variables used factor analysis—a technique which focuses on characterizing continuous latent variables by analyzing sets of continuous (or sometimes dichotomous) observed indicators. The widespread use of regression analysis undoubtedly contributed to the popularity of this method, since factor analysis could be used to reduce many observed variables to only a few latent factors, and the predicted factor scores could then be used in regression analyses. Jöreskog's (Jöreskog and Sörbom 1979) contributions to the analysis of covariance structures and linear structural equation models provide efficient methods for estimating parameters for models in which continuous latent variables are characterized by analyzing the relationships among continuous observed variables.

Until recently, however, social researchers have not had similar techniques for analyzing discrete (categorical) data. Interest in such methods for discrete data has increased for two reasons. One is the realization that many variables—both observable and unobservable—are not continuous. For example, the variable of interest might be a *typology* constructed from a combination of values of several constituent variables. Typologies allow analysts to focus their attention on only those combinations that actually *do* occur, rather than examining all combinations of constituent variables that *can* occur (Stinchcombe 1968, 41-47). Such variables are inherently categorical and can greatly improve theories and analyses. A second reason is that observed variables may be *measured* at either the nominal or ordinal level of measurement. Indeed, well over half of the variables available in several of the most widely analyzed social science data sets are scored as categorical data (Clogg 1979).

Recent developments now provide a range of analytic techniques for parametric causal analysis among nominal and ordinal level data. Developments in linear probability, log-linear, logit, and probit analyses, as well as several other approaches, provide current researchers with a variety of powerful techniques for analyzing causal relationships among ordinal and nominal level-dependent and -independent variables (see, e.g., Goodman 1972; Haberman 1979; Maddala 1983; Aldrich and Nelson 1984). Consequently, researchers are gaining an increasing capacity to select analytic techniques that conform to the requirements of both their theory and the nature of their measures.

In this paper we examine the use of the latent class model for analyzing latent variables with discrete data. As we will see, latent class analysis is a method for studying categorically scored variables that is analogous to modern factor analysis. Moreover, the latent class model requires neither the often violated assumption of multivariate normality nor the assumption of continuity of measurement.

WHAT IS LATENT CLASS ANALYSIS?

Lazarsfeld coined the term *latent structure analysis* to describe the use of mathematical models for characterizing latent variables in the analysis of attitudinal measures from survey research (Henry 1983). Lazarsfeld included factor analysis as the latent structure method for characterizing continuous latent variables (factors) based on continuous observed variables. Latent *class* analysis, then, can be considered a qualitative data analog to factor analysis which enables researchers to empirically identify discrete latent variables from two or more discrete observed variables (Green 1951, 1952). Two additional techniques complete the array of latent structure methods: latent trait analysis enables the characterization of continuous latent variables from discrete observed variables, and latent profile analysis enables the characterization of discrete latent variables from continuous observed variables.

The comparison of the latent class model with the factor model is useful in as much as each method enables researchers to explore the latent structures among a set of observed variables (exploratory analysis) and to test hypotheses about the latent structures among a set of observed variables (confirmatory analysis). Unlike the factor model, however, a latent variable characterized by the latent class model may be either unidimensional—e.g., to analyze the scalability of a set of observed categorical items into ordinal measures of latent variables—or multidimensional—e.g., to empirically characterize typological classifications from a set of observed discrete measures. Recent developments in latent class analysis make it possible to analyze the same observed variables to compare the latent variables identified in multiple populations (Clogg and Goodman 1984, 1985, 1986). This flexibility makes it possible for analysts to test directly whether a set of observed measures defines a unidimensional or multidimensional latent variable within a population, and whether the latent variable is invariant over multiple populations.

In its most general form, latent class analysis makes possible the characterization of a multidimensional discrete latent variable from a cross-classification of two or more observed categorical variables. Latent class analysis enables the researcher to identify a set of mutually exclusive latent classes that account for the distribution of cases that occur within a crosstabulation of observed discrete variables. One important use of latent class analysis, then, is for the analysis of typologies—either as a method for empirically characterizing a set of latent types within a set of observed indicators, or as a method for testing whether a theoretically posited typology adequately represents the data. Given the significant role played by typologies in social science theory and research, and the difficulties encountered with other data analytic methods employed in identifying and testing latent typologies, latent class analysis provides an extremely important method for the social sciences.

We can illustrate the general form of latent class analysis with a reanalysis of the example of universalistic and particularistic values data examined earlier by Toby and Stouffer (1951), Lazarsfeld and Henry (1968), and Goodman (1974a, 1975, 1979). In the study, 216 Harvard and Radcliff undergraduates were asked in 1950 how they would respond in four role-conflict situations, such as the following:

Your friend is riding in a car which you are driving, and you hit a pedestrian. He knows that you are going at least 35 miles an hour in a 20-mile-an-hour zone. There are no other witnesses. Your lawyer says that if your friend testifies under oath that the speed was only 20 miles an hour, it may save you from serious consequences. What right have you to expect him to protect you? (*Universalistic response:* I have no right as a friend to expect him to testify to the lower figure.)

The other scenarios include the respondents' expectations from (1) a physician friend to "shade doubts" about physical examination diagnoses for an insurance policy with the doctor's employer, (2) a drama critic friend to "go easy on a review" of a bad play in which all of the respondent's savings are invested, and (3) a board of directors friend to "tip-off" the respondent about financially ruinous, though secret, company information. The actual data from the ($2 \times 2 \times 2 \times 2 =$) 16-fold crosstabulation are reported in the earlier cited works and are not reported here.

The proportions reported in Table 1.1 are the results of a latent class analysis of the 16-celled crosstabulation of the four survey items. Momentarily setting aside the specifics of how we arrive at these results and how well the results compare to the actual data (it is quite a good "fit"), we see that there are two types of probabilities in the latent class analysis model. The first type of probability indicates the likelihood of a universalitic response by respondents in each of the two classes. For example, we see that respondents in the first class (Universalistic) have a high probability of giving the universalistic response to the four situations (.769 to .993), while respondents in the second class (Particularistic) have a high probability of giving a universalistic response to only one of the four situations (.714 for Auto Passenger Friends). The second type of probability indicates the relative frequency of each of the two types (classes) of respondents in the population.

Using the information in Table 1.1, we can classify each of the 216 respondents as expressing either Universalistic or Particularistic values. While Stouffer and Toby (1951) obtained these responses from Harvard and Radcliff undergraduates in 1950, if

Table 1.1: Probability of Universalistic Response and Relative
Frequency for the Two-Class Model

| Observed Variables | Respondent Type | |
	Universalistic (I)	Particularistic (II)
Auto Passanger Friend	.993	.714
Insurance Doctor Friend	.939	.329
Drama Critic Friend	.926	.354
Board of Directors Friend	.769	.132
Latent class relative frequency	.2797	.7204

we had responses to these four questions from a sample of respondents in other groups, say graduate students from these institutions in 1950 or undergraduates in 1980, the latent class model could be used to compare the latent structures of Univeralism-Particularism in the two (or more) groups; or, we could use the latent class model to examine the scalability of the four items. As we will see below, the latent class model can be used to examine a variety of issues in the analysis of discrete data.

GENERAL OUTLINE OF PRESENTATION

In Chapter 2 we examine the logic and the formal model of latent structure analysis. The reader, initially, may wish to skip this chapter and go to the examples presented in the later chapters. A thorough understanding of latent class analysis, however, will require mastery of the model presented in the second chapter. In Chapter 3 we examine some applications of latent class analysis, presenting both the logic and interpretations of a typological analysis; also, we distinguish between exploratory and confirmatory uses of the latent class model. In Chapter 4 we focus on the use of the latent structure model for analyzing the scalability of dichotomous and ordinally scored variables. In Chapter 5 we examine the use of simultaneous latent class analysis for comparing the latent structures of different populations.

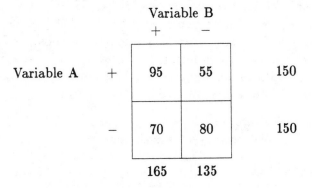

Table 2.1: Hypothetical Two-Item Crosstabulation

2. LATENT CLASS ANALYSIS

Latent class analysis is a technique for analyzing relationships in categorical data; that is, relationships among variables scored at either the nominal or ordinal level of measurement. The fundamental logic of latent class analysis can be seen from a relatively simple crosstabulation of data such as the one presented in Table 2.1.

These data indicate that variables A and B are not independent of one another. That is, the information in Table 2.1 suggests that in this sample these variables are too interrelated for us to attribute the observed pattern to chance alone ($\chi^2 = 8.42$ with 1 degree of freedom, $p < .01$). The chi-square test here is calculated in the usual manner in which the estimate of the expected proportion $(\hat{P}_{ij})$ in each cell is computed as the product of the marginal proportions of the appropriate row and column:

$$\hat{P}_{ij} = \hat{P}_{i.} \times \hat{P}_{.j} \qquad (2.1)$$

and the estimate of the expected cell frequency $(\hat{F}_{ij})$ is computed as

$$\hat{F}_{ij} = N \times \hat{P}_{ij} \qquad (2.2)$$

where variable A is indexed by $i = 1, 2$; variable B is indexed by $j = 1, 2$; and N is the sample size.[1]

Interpretations of relationships between two or more variables, such as that presented in Table 2.1, typically take one of two forms.

The first form of interpretation involves the idea of causality—that is, the analyst is inclined to suggest that either variable A or variable B is causally prior (i.e., independent) to the other (i.e., dependent). The second form of interpretation does not involve the issue of causal ordering. Rosenberg refers to this form of relationship as a symmetrical relationship. Symmetrical relationships, he argues, can be separated into five types (1968, 3-7):

Alternative indicators of the same concept are the type of symmetrical relationships that most concerns researchers in scale analysis—several survey items may be highly interrelated because all are indicators of the same underlying phenomenon (e.g., depression, alienation, anomie).

Parts of a common "system" or "complex" represent the type of symmetrical relationship in which items are interrelated due to common practice—the association between martini drinking and opera attendance, Rosenberg suggests, is due to a common complex we refer to as "style of life."

Functional interdependence of elements, involves the interrelatedness of variables that are likely to be jointly present (or absent) due to their significance for the system under study; thus, in organizations with formal, abstract, impersonal rules, one also usually finds administrative rules, acts, and decisions recorded in writing; in organizations where one of these sets of features is absent, the other also tends to be absent.

Effects of a common cause, involve the interrelatedness of variables due to some common causally prior variable; thus, among various nations we may observe an inverse correlation between the annual per capita kilowatt output and birth rates, though we are likely to view both as effects of the level of development or technology, and not electrical output as an effect of birth rate or birth rate as an effect of electrical output.

Fortuitous relationships are those in which two or more variables represent coincidental correlations that have no logical relationship, such as the "rough chronological relationship between rock 'n' roll music and the onset of the space age."

While Clogg (1981a) has provided a detailed presentation for using latent class techniques in causal analyses, latent class analysis has not yet found widespread use with this type of interpretation. Since causal interpretations require more complex latent class models, we will defer discussion of this type of interpretation until a later chapter. We begin the discussion of latent class analysis, then, according to its most general and widespread use—as a method for examining symmetrical relationships among discretely scored (categorical) variables, in which Rosenberg's five types of interrelations represent several of the interpretations available in latent class analysis. A researcher's choice of one interpretation over another depends on the dictates of theory and logic. Researchers using latent class methods to analyze scales are likely to interpret relationships between measures as the result of their being alternative indicators of the same concept. A detailed examination of the use of latent class analytic techniques in analyzing scales is presented in Chapter 4. The interpretations of symmetrical relationships as parts of a common complex, as due to functional interdependence, or as effects of a common cause are used in the study of typologies. The analysis of typologies with latent class analytic techniques represents the most general form of the latent class model; this general model provides a focus for much of the explanation that follows.

Recent developments in latent class methods demonstrate that this analytic method also provides insight into the comparative analysis of scales and typologies in different populations (Clogg and Goodman 1984, 1985, 1986). Consequently, when different populations represent different social groups (e.g., regional, racial, political), latent class analysis methods can be used to compare the scale characteristics and typologies based on identical measures used with each of the social groups. When we identify latent classes at two or more times in the same population of study (e.g., such as when survey researchers analyze several cross-sections in the study of trends), latent class analysts can study historical changes in the scale characteristics and typologies identified using identical measures at different times for the same population. Latent class analysis also can be used to gain new insights into a variety of social processes, such as intergenerational occupational mobility or interreligious marriage (Clogg 1981b; Marsden 1985). Finally, the realization that symmetrical relationships between variables may be fortuitous underscores Mandansky's caution: "it may happen that the ... latent classes have no reasonable interpretation, let alone the hoped for interpretation" (1968, 34).

LOCAL INDEPENDENCE

The data reported in Table 2.1 suggest that variables A and B are not independent of one another, since the goodness-of-fit χ^2 statistic for testing independence for these data (8.42) is significant well beyond the .01 level. For expository purposes, we will assume that the relationship presented in Table 2.1 represents Srole's (1956) questions "In spite of what people say, the lot of the average man is getting worse, not better" and "These days a person doesn't really know whom he can count on" as indicators of anomie. Thus the assumption that the relationship in Table 2.1 is symmetrical means that we do not believe that peoples' feelings on the "lot of the average man" (variable A) cause their feelings about "who to count on" (variable B), or vice versa. Instead, we are likely to believe that the observed relationship between the answers to these two questions is attributable to the common factor we refer to as "anomie" (variable C). That is, we hypothesize that persons experiencing anomie are likely to answer affirmatively to both of the questions, and that persons who are not anomic are likely to answer negatively to both questions; anomie is said to "explain" the relationship between feelings toward the "lot of the average man" and feelings about "who to count on"—variable C explains the relationship between variables A and B.

If we assume for the moment that we have such a measure of anomie—a variable C—then we might conceivably find a distribution such as that presented in Table 2.2. At each level of variable C, the variables A and B are independent of one another ($\chi^2 = 0.0$ with 2 degrees of freedom), where the expected proportions are calculated as:

$$\hat{P}_{ijk} = \hat{P}_{ik}^{\bar{A}C} \times \hat{P}_{jk}^{\bar{B}C} \times \hat{P}_{k}^{C} \qquad (2.3)$$

where $\hat{P}_{ik}^{\bar{A}C}$ is the estimate of the conditional probability of a case being at level i of variable A given that it is at level k of variable C; $\hat{P}_{jk}^{\bar{B}C}$ is the estimate of the conditional probability of B given the level of C; and $\hat{P}_k^C$ is the estimate of the probability of a case being at level k of variable C.

Although this notation may appear somewhat complicated at first, it follows a rather straightforward logic. The circumflexes ("hats") above the P's indicate that the probabilities are sample estimates, and are relatively common in many statistical expressions. The upper "bar" (e.g., $\bar{A}C$, $\bar{B}C$), on the other hand, is somewhat less common in other statistical approaches. The bar notation is used to indicate that the probability is a *conditional* probability—that is, the estimated probability of the barred variable is calculated within the levels of the nonbarred variable(s). Thus, the estimated probability $\hat{P}_{11}^{\bar{A}C}$ is calculated as the probability that respondents within level 1 of variable C (the nonbarred variable) choose response 1 for variable A (the barred variable). For example, from Table 2.2 we estimate the probability that anomic respondents feel that the lot of the average man is getting worse ($\hat{P}_{11}^{\bar{A}C}$) is .667 (= 100/150) and estimate the probability that they do not know who they count on is ($\hat{P}_{11}^{\bar{B}C}$) is .800 (= 120/150); the estimated probability that nonanomic respondents feel that the lot of the average man is getting worse ($\hat{P}_{12}^{\bar{A}C}$) is .333 (= 50/150) and the estimated probability that they do not know who to count on ($\hat{P}_{12}^{\bar{B}C}$) is .300 (= 45/150). Thus the probability that any given anomic respondent answers affirmatively to both questions is equal to the product of their estimated (conditional) probability of responding affirmatively to variable A ($\hat{P}_{11}^{\bar{A}C}$) and their estimated (conditional) probability of responding affirmatively to variable B ($\hat{P}_{11}^{\bar{B}C}$). The joint probability that any given respondent feels that the lot of the average man is getting worse, does not know who to count on, and suffers from anomie is .2668 ($\hat{P}_{11}^{\bar{A}C} \times \hat{P}_{11}^{\bar{B}C} \times \hat{P}_1^C = .667 \times .800 \times .500$). To calculate the expected frequencies, we multiply $\hat{P}_{ijk}$ by the total number of cases:

$$\hat{F}_{ijk} = N \times \hat{P}_{ijk} = N \times \hat{P}_{ik}^{\bar{A}C} \times \hat{P}_{jk}^{\bar{B}C} \times \hat{P}_k^C \qquad (2.4)$$

Table 2.2: Hypothetical Three-Item Crosstabulation

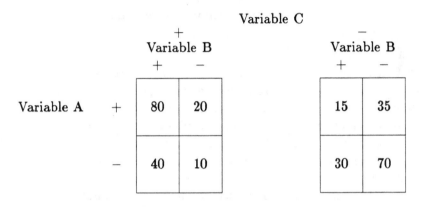

where $\hat{F}_{ijk}$ represents the estimated expected number of observations in each (i, j, k) cell of the table, and N represents the total number of cases.

For the example data presented in Table 2.2, each of the observed cell entries is exactly equal to the expected frequencies calculated by using equation 2.4 (i.e., $f_{ijk} = \hat{F}_{ijk}$), in which variables A and B are hypothesized to be independent of one another, conditional on the level of variable C. Lazarsfeld and Henry (1968) refer to this condition as "local independence"; that is, when the relationships observed among a set of variables are found to be zero within the categories of some other variable, this set of variables is said to be locally independent with respect to this explanatory variable. Thus, from the data reported in Table 2.2, we see that variables A and B are locally independent of one another with respect to variable C.

The criterion of local independence, then, provides a method for determining whether relationships among a set of observed measures are due to some unmeasured explanatory variable. When a set of interrelated variables are found to be locally independent within categories of some additional variable, we say that the additional variable "explains" the observed relationships—that the additional variable represents the true variable of interest, and that once it is considered all of the other measures are unrelated.

THE FORMAL LATENT CLASS MODEL

The data presented in Table 2.2 show that we have measured a variable (C) that explains the symmetrical relationship between variables A and B—often, however, we are not so fortunate as to have measured that variable. The object of latent class analysis is to define a latent variable—specifically, a set of classes within which the manifest variables are locally independent. If such a variable can be defined, then its classes are taken to represent either the latent types or the categorical scale locations of the variable as they are defined by the measured variables within the sampled population.

Before proceeding to a discussion of the characteristics of latent classes and how they can be estimated from observed data, we first return to a discussion of the data presented in Table 2.2. Recalling the earlier discussion, it was noted that within categories of variable C, variables A and B are completely independent of one another. This relationship is expressed in equation 2.3 by stating that the proportion of each of the i, j, k combinations is the product of the conditional probability of variable A $(P_{ik}^{\bar{A}C})$, the conditional probability of variable B $(P_{jk}^{\bar{B}C})$, and the probability of falling in the particular category of variable C (P_k^C). When the variable that designates the explanatory categories is not measured (i.e., when "variable C" is latent), the probabilities are symbolized as π, and the latent classes are designated as a latent variable X with T classes (levels). Thus we would express an equation parallel to equation 2.3 as:

$$\pi_{ijt}^{ABX} = \pi_{it}^{\bar{A}X} \times \pi_{jt}^{\bar{B}X} \times \pi_t^X \qquad (2.5)$$

where π_{ijt}^{ABX} is the probability that a randomly selected case will be located in the i, j, t cell, $\pi_{it}^{\bar{A}X}$ is the conditional probability that a case in class t of the latent variable (X) will be located at level i of variable A, $\pi_{jt}^{\bar{B}X}$ is the conditional probability of being at level j of variable B, and π_t^X is the probability of a randomly selected case being at level t of the latent variable X. More generally, then, equation 2.5 can be expressed as:

$$\pi_{ij\cdots mt}^{AB\cdots EX} = \pi_{it}^{\bar{A}X} \times \pi_{jt}^{\bar{B}X} \times \cdots \times \pi_{mt}^{\bar{E}X} \times \pi_t^X \qquad (2.6)$$

which states that the symmetrical relationships among the observed measures are locally independent within the latent classes—that is, that the probability of occurrence in each of the cells of the $i, j, \ldots, m, t$ crosstabulation is expected to equal the product of the conditional probabilities $(\pi_{it}^{\bar{A}X}, \pi_{jt}^{\bar{B}C}$, etc.) and the probability associated with being in any particular class of the latent variable X (π_t^X).

The latent class probabilities and conditional probabilities are the two fundamental quantities of latent class analysis. Below, we examine the method, first presented by Goodman (1974a, 1974b), for obtaining maximum likelihood estimates of the conditional and latent class probabilities. Throughout most of this discussion we will consider the instance in which three observed variables are used to estimate the latent variable. That is, we will consider the case where

$$\pi_{ijkt}^{ABCX} = \pi_{it}^{\bar{A}X} \times \pi_{jt}^{\bar{B}X} \times \pi_{kt}^{\bar{C}X} \times \pi_t^X \qquad (2.7)$$

All of the discussion can, of course, be expanded to cases where more than three observed variables are used in the analysis. Before examining the estimation procedure, however, we will briefly discuss the interpretation of the two essential parameters.

Latent Class Probabilities

The latent class probabilities (π_t^X) describe the distribution of classes (levels) of the latent variable within which the observed measures are (locally) independent of one another. Thus there are two important aspects of the latent class probabilities: the *number* of classes and the *relative sizes* of these classes. The number of classes (T) in the latent variable (X) represents the number of latent types defined by the latent class model for the observed crosstabulation; in scale analysis each class represents a separate, identifiable location on the scale. Thus, for example, if the latent variable has three classes, the population can be described as being either three "types" or three levels of an underlying (latent) continuum. The minimum number of identifiable classes in a latent variable is two, since a latent variable with only a single latent class (i.e., $T = 1$) is equivalent to finding independence among the observed variables.

The relative size of each of the T classes also provides significant information for the interpretation of the latent class probabilities. The relative sizes of the latent class probabilities indicate whether the population is relatively evenly distributed among the T classes, or whether some of the latent classes represent relatively large segments of the population while other classes represent relatively small segments. The sum of the latent class probabilities (π_t^X) over all T latent classes of the latent variable (X) must equal one:

$$\sum_t \pi_t^X = 1.00 \qquad (2.8)$$

Later, we will see that the relative sizes of the latent class probabilities are also very useful for comparing latent structures in two or more populations. When the relative sizes of the latent classes differ in two (or more) populations which have similar latent structures, the differences represent distributional heterogeneity of the set of types (or levels of the scale) between the populations. When the "different populations" represent observations on the same population at two or more times, these differences represent changes in the distribution of the population across the classes over time (i.e., historical trends).

Conditional Probabilities

The second essential type of latent class parameter—the conditional probability—is comparable to the factor loading in factor analysis. These parameters represent the probabilities of an individual in class t of the latent variable (X) being at a particular level of the observed variables. Using our earlier example from Table 2.2, the conditional probability $P_{11}^{\bar{B}C}$ represents the probability of an anomic individual feeling that the lot of the average man is getting worse (i.e., persons at level 1 of variable C), and $P_{12}^{\bar{B}C}$ represents the probability of a nonanomic individual feeling that the lot of the average man is getting worse. Similarly, the conditional probabilities $P_{11}^{\bar{A}C}$ and $P_{12}^{\bar{A}C}$ are the probabilities of not knowing who to count on associated with anomic and nonanomic respondents, respectively. Thus, when the type variable is unobserved (e.g., when the anomie variable C is a latent variable X), latent class analysis enables the researcher to identify the conditional probabilities $(\pi_{it}^{\bar{A}X}, \pi_{jt}^{\bar{B}X}, \ldots, \pi_{mt}^{\bar{E}X})$.

For each of the T classes of the latent variable there is a set of conditional probabilities for each of the observed variables. For example, if three observed variables have been used to define the latent classes, each of the classes will have three sets of conditional probabilities $(\pi_{it}^{\bar{A}X}, \pi_{jt}^{\bar{B}X}, \pi_{kt}^{\bar{C}X})$. Since each of the observed variables can be either dichotomous or polytomous, the number of distinct conditional probabilities for each of the observed variables is equal to the number of levels measured for that variable. That is, if an observed variable has two levels (e.g., feels the lot of the average man is getting worse, does not feel that the lot of the average man is getting worse), there will be two associated probabilities: $\pi_{1t}^{\bar{A}X}$, which represents the conditional probability that persons of class t feel that the lot of the average man is getting worse, and $\pi_{2t}^{\bar{A}X}$, which represents the conditional probability that persons of class t do not feel the lot of the average man is getting worse. Similarly, if there are three observed variables, there are $I + J + K$ distinct conditional probabilities for each of the T classes of the latent variable (X). We should note that within each of the T latent classes the conditional probabilities for each of the observed variables sum to 1.00:

$$\sum_i \pi_{it}^{\bar{A}X} = \sum_j \pi_{jt}^{\bar{B}X} = \sum_k \pi_{kt}^{\bar{C}X} = 1.00 \qquad (2.9)$$

Consequently, within each latent class the observations have a specific probability of being at a given level of the observed variables. Since the conditional probabilities for each observed variable must sum to 1.0 within each latent class, there is one redundant conditional probability for each observed variable within each latent class. For example, in an analysis with three observed variables, there are $(I-1) + (J-1) + (K-1)$ conditional probabilities which need to be identified for each of the (T) latent classes.

The conditional probabilities enable us to characterize the nature of the types defined by each of the latent classes and hence the nature of the latent variable. Within each of the latent classes, the conditional probabilities indicate whether observations in class t are likely or unlikely to have characteristics of each of the observed variables. Thus, if we were investigating anomie and estimated that in one class 90% of the members reported feeling that the lot of the average man is getting worse and that 80% reported not knowing who to count on, while in the other class we estimated the respective percents to be 30% and 25%, we might be inclined to typify the first latent class as anomic and the second latent class as nonanomic. It is because of this usage that conditional probabilities have been described as analogous to factor scores in factor analysis.

MAXIMUM LIKELIHOOD ESTIMATION

In this section we will examine the procedure, first outlined by Goodman (1974a, 1974b, 1979), for obtaining maximum likelihood estimates (MLEs) of the conditional and latent class probabilities. Unlike the earlier proposed determinantal methods for estimating these latent class quantities (see, e.g., Anderson 1954; Lazarsfeld and Henry 1968), Goodman's maximum likelihood procedure provides estimates that cannot lie outside of the allowed interval (i.e., 0.0–1.0). Although McHugh (1956) had suggested an efficient method for latent class analysis, Goodman's procedure is simpler and more general—as we will see below when we discuss restricted latent class models. Consequently, Goodman's estimators provide a crucial breakthrough beyond the earlier approaches for the estimation of latent class parameters. Goodman's estimation procedure has been implemented in a readily accessible computer program MLLSA (Maximum Likelihood Latent Structure Analysis) (Clogg 1977), which is documented in Appendix A.

Although the latent class model is somewhat more complex than the two-variable independence model, the necessity of faithfully representing the original observed relationships is the same. It is only possible to accept the latent class model—and thus the defined latent variable—if the model yields expectations that deviate from the observed data only within the limits of chance variation (e.g., if the χ^2 statistic is small relative to the degrees of freedom). To obtain the maximum likelihood estimates for the specified latent class model, we begin by modifying equation 2.7 by adding circumflexes to denote that these latent class parameters are maximum likelihood estimates:

$$\hat{\pi}_{ijkt}^{ABCX} = \hat{\pi}_{it}^{\bar{A}X} \times \hat{\pi}_{jt}^{\bar{B}X} \times \hat{\pi}_{kt}^{\bar{C}X} \times \hat{\pi}_{t}^{X} \qquad (2.10)$$

Here we see that equation 2.10 is quite similar to equation 2.7, except now we note that the probability of an observation being located in the i, j, k, t cell is a maximum likelihood estimate if it is the product of the MLE conditional probabilities and the MLE latent class probabilities. If we sum equation 2.10 over all T classes of the latent variable, we obtain the MLE joint probability associated with each of the $(I \times J \times K)$ levels of the observed variables.

$$\hat{\pi}_{ijk} = \sum_{t} \hat{\pi}_{ijkt}^{ABCX} \qquad (2.11)$$

This equation provides us with the MLE expected probabilities for the latent class model, much as equation 2.1 provides us with the expected probabilities for the two-variable independence model. Thus equation 2.11 is a very important equation—it provides us with the expected values with which we can test the fit of the latent class model. As with the usual chi-square test, if the expected values are within the limits of chance variation from the observed values, we can accept the conditional and latent class probabilities of equation 2.10 as faithful representations of the observed data. If the χ^2 statistic is too large relative to the degrees of freedom, then the expected value exceeds the limits of chance variation and we must reject the latent class model specified in 2.10.

If we divide equation 2.10 by equation 2.11, we obtain the MLE probability that an observation at level i, j, k of the observed variables will be at level t of the latent variable.

$$\hat{\pi}_{ijkt}^{ABC\bar{X}} = \hat{\pi}_{ijkt}^{ABCX} / \hat{\pi}_{ijk} \qquad (2.12)$$

This equation provides us with the probability that observations in the ijk cell of the three variable crosstabulation will be at level t of the latent variable. Later we will see that this probability can be used to assign observations to the T classes of the latent varible. Goodman (1974a, 1979) notes that when we have a set of observed proportions p_{ijk} of individuals who are at the (i, j, k) levels of a crosstabulation of observed variables (A, B, C), standard methods can be used to prove that the maximum likelihood estimates of equations 2.9–2.11 satisfy the following set of equations (see also Haberman 1974, 1979):

$$\hat{\pi}_t^X = \sum_{ijk} p_{ijk} \hat{\pi}_{ijkt}^{ABC\bar{X}} \tag{2.13}$$

$$\hat{\pi}_{it}^{\bar{A}X} = \frac{\sum_{jk} p_{ijk} \hat{\pi}_{ijkt}^{ABC\bar{X}}}{\hat{\pi}_t^X} \tag{2.14}$$

$$\hat{\pi}_{jt}^{\bar{B}X} = \frac{\sum_{ik} p_{ijk} \hat{\pi}_{ijkt}^{ABC\bar{X}}}{\hat{\pi}_t^X} \tag{2.15}$$

$$\hat{\pi}_{kt}^{\bar{C}X} = \frac{\sum_{ij} p_{ijk} \hat{\pi}_{ijkt}^{ABC\bar{X}}}{\hat{\pi}_t^X} \tag{2.16}$$

In the next section we will examine the iterative process through which the above set of equations can yield maximum likelihood estimates of the conditional and latent class probabilities for the latent class model. Although more technical than the preceding discussion, this final section will be useful to those wishing to write their own computer programs for finding maximum likelihood estimates for the latent class models.

Iterative Proportional Scaling of Parameters

The analyst provides the initial, or start, estimates of the conditional and latent class probabilities of the model expressed in equation 2.10. The initial estimates from these equations can then be used to find new estimates of the conditional and latent class probabilities by using variations of equations 2.9 and 2.13–2.15. This iterative procedure, the so-called EM algorithm (Dempster

24

et al. 1977), produces maximum likelihood estimates (Goodman 1974a, 1979). Letting $\bar{\pi}_t^X$, $\bar{\pi}_{it}^{\bar{A}X}$, $\bar{\pi}_{jt}^{\bar{B}X}$, and $\bar{\pi}_{kt}^{\bar{C}X}$ denote the start values for the corresponding model parameters, we obtain an initial value $\bar{\pi}_{ijkt}^{ABCX}$ for $\hat{\pi}_{ijkt}^{ABCX}$:

$$\bar{\pi}_{ijkt}^{ABCX} = \bar{\pi}_t^X \bar{\pi}_{it}^{\bar{A}X} \bar{\pi}_{jt}^{\bar{B}X} \bar{\pi}_{kt}^{\bar{C}X} \qquad (2.17)$$

This value is used to obtain initial values $\bar{\pi}_{ijk}$ and $\bar{\pi}_{ijkt}^{ABC\bar{X}}$ for $\hat{\pi}_{ijk}$ and $\hat{\pi}_{ijkt}^{ABC\bar{X}}$:

$$\bar{\pi}_{ijk} = \sum_{t=1}^{T} \bar{\pi}_{ijkt}^{ABCX} \qquad (2.18)$$

$$\bar{\pi}_{ijkt}^{ABC\bar{X}} = \frac{\bar{\pi}_{ijkt}^{ABCX}}{\bar{\pi}_{ijk}} \qquad (2.19)$$

Using the observed p_{ijk}'s we obtain a new trial value $\bar{\pi}_t^X$ for $\hat{\pi}_t^X$:

$$\bar{\pi}_t^X = \sum_{ijk} p_{ijk} \bar{\pi}_{ijkt}^{ABC\bar{X}} \qquad (2.20)$$

This can be used to obtain new trial values $\bar{\pi}_{it}^{\bar{A}X}$, $\bar{\pi}_{jt}^{\bar{B}X}$, and $\bar{\pi}_{kt}^{\bar{C}X}$:

$$\bar{\pi}_{it}^{\bar{A}X} = \frac{\sum_{jk} p_{ijk} \bar{\pi}_{ijkt}^{ABC\bar{X}}}{\bar{\pi}_t^X} \qquad (2.21)$$

$$\bar{\pi}_{jt}^{\bar{B}X} = \frac{\sum_{ik} p_{ijk} \bar{\pi}_{ijkt}^{ABC\bar{X}}}{\bar{\pi}_t^X} \qquad (2.22)$$

$$\bar{\pi}_{kt}^{\bar{C}X} = \frac{\sum_{ij} p_{ijk} \bar{\pi}_{ijkt}^{ABC\bar{X}}}{\hat{\pi}_t^X} \qquad (2.23)$$

The iterative process begins with initial trial values for the latent class probabilities and the conditional probabilities ($\bar{\pi}_t^X$, $\bar{\pi}_{it}^{\bar{A}X}$, $\bar{\pi}_{jt}^{\bar{B}C}$, $\bar{\pi}_{kt}^{\bar{C}X}$) for equation 2.17; the estimate from the left-hand side of 2.17 is then used to obtain new estimates for 2.18 and 2.19; and these estimates are in turn used to obtain new estimates of the latent class and conditional probabilities from equations 2.20–2.23.

The new estimates of the latent class and conditional probabilities obtained in equations 2.20–2.23 are then returned to equation 2.17 to obtain new estimates of each of the probabilities.

There are two methods that can be used to halt this iterative process of estimation and reestimation of probabilities. First, the analyst can determine how many iterations he or she is willing to complete. The disadvantage of this approach is that the estimates may still be changing substantially from iteration to iteration. In the second method the estimates of the latent class and conditional probabilities obtained from equations 2.20–2.23 are compared with those of 2.17 at the end of each iteration; if the differences in each of the estimates is less than a predetermined amount (*tolerance*), the process stops, and equation 2.17 can be used to test the fit of the obtained estimates to the originally observed data.

There are three points that need to be made regarding the estimation of conditional and latent class probabilities. First, there might be more than one solution to the likelihood equations; that is, there may exist more than one set of conditional and latent class probabilities for any specified number of T latent classes. In other words, the maximum likelihood estimates may represent a local, rather than the global, maximum. Thus the analyst needs to try more than a single set of initial values in equation 2.17. In practice, this presents very little problem, since each of the sets of initial values typically results in the same final estimates.

The second point is that the number of estimable parameters is limited by the available degrees of freedom in the crosstabulation of the observed variables ($[I \times J \times K] - 1$). In the model specified in equation 2.17—which we will refer to as the *unrestricted* model with *all parameters identified*—the number of estimated parameters is

$$(T-1)+T(I-1)+T(J-1)+T(K-1) = (I+J+K-2)T-1 \quad (2.24)$$

That is, we are estimating $T - 1$ latent class probabilities and $(I - 1) + (J - 1) + (K - 1)$ conditional probabilities for each of the T latent classes (recalling the requirement of equations 2.8 and 2.9 that the latent class and conditional probabilities sum to 1.00). The degrees of freedom for the chi-square tests is computed as:

$$DF = (IJK - 1) - [(I + J + K - 2)T - 1] \quad (2.25)$$

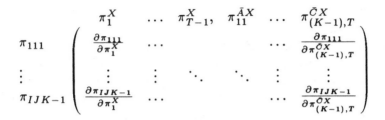

$$
\pi_{111} \quad
\begin{array}{c}
 \\
\pi_{IJK-1}
\end{array}
\left(
\begin{array}{ccccccc}
\dfrac{\partial \pi_{111}}{\partial \pi_1^X} & \cdots & & & \cdots & \dfrac{\partial \pi_{111}}{\partial \pi_{(K-1),T}^{\bar{C}X}} \\
\vdots & \vdots & \ddots & \ddots & \vdots & \vdots \\
\dfrac{\partial \pi_{IJK-1}}{\partial \pi_1^X} & \cdots & & & \cdots & \dfrac{\partial \pi_{IJK-1}}{\partial \pi_{(K-1),T}^{\bar{C}X}}
\end{array}
\right)
$$

Figure 2.1: Partial Derivatives Matrix for Assessing
Model Identifiability

Thus, only when there is a positive number of degrees of freedom can the model of equation 2.17 be both estimated and tested.

Third, a multiplicity of parameter values or estimates may be associated with a given solution (i.e., the identification problem). Unfortunately, there are models for which the results to equation 2.25 are positive but for which no set of unique model parameters exist. A simple example is in the instance of four dichotomous observed variables and a three-class latent variable $(T = 3)$, where the results of equation 2.25 are positive $(df = 1)$ but the model is not identified (Goodman 1974a).

A necessary and sufficient condition for determining the *local identifiability* of a latent-class model is also provided by Goodman (1974a). This involves determining the rank order of a $(IJK - 1)$ by $([I + J + K - 2]T - 1)$ matrix of partial derivatives of the nonredundant observed probabilities with respect to the nonredundant model parameters (Figure 2.1). In this matrix each cell element is a partial derivative of each row element with respect to the corresponding column element, e.g.,

$$
\frac{\partial \pi_{ijk}}{\partial \pi_t^X} = \pi_{it}^{\bar{A}X}\pi_{jt}^{\bar{B}X}\pi_{kt}^{\bar{C}X} - \pi_{iT}^{\bar{A}X}\pi_{jT}^{\bar{B}X}\pi_{kT}^{\bar{C}X}. \tag{2.26}
$$

To be locally identified, the matrix in Figure 2.1 must be of full column rank, equal to $(I + J + K - 2)T - 1$. In other words, there must be no linearly dependent columns. Calculation of the rank of this matrix is performed by the MLLSA program and is reported along with the parameter estimates.

Unidentified models can be made identifiable by imposing restrictions on one or more of the model parameters. When restrictions are imposed, the right-hand side of equation 2.25 no longer reflects the number of nonredundant model parameters to be estimated. Consequently, restricting the model means that we must decrement the right-hand side of equation 2.25 by the number of nonredundant restrictions imposed. We will explore models with restrictions more thoroughly below, but first we examine latent class models without restrictions.

3. ESTIMATING LATENT CATEGORICAL VARIABLES

As we noted in the previous two chapters, the most general form of latent class analysis permits us to characterize a nominal level latent variable from a crosstabulation of two or more ordinal or nominal level observed variables. Identifying such latent variables holds the potential for greatly improving research, since it enables researchers to focus their attention on the set of T classes (or types) identified in the analysis, rather than consider each of the observed variables separately or all of the possible combinations of the observed measures. Thus, like factor analysis, latent class analysis is a useful method for data reduction, increasing the interpretability of data based on several different variables. Latent class analysis also enables researchers to characterize the *structure* of the latent typology by examining the conditional probabilities for each of the observed variables in each of the latent classes; for example, by noting a propensity toward not knowing who to trust and feeling the lot of the average man is getting worse among persons in one class of the latent variable, and opposing tendencies among persons in the other class, the researcher can interpret the nature of the latent types.

As is the case in factor analysis, it is useful to distinquish between *exploratory* and *confirmatory* latent class analysis. In exploratory latent class analysis researchers attempt to identify a set of latent classes from a set of observed measures—no attempt is made to test any hypothesis regarding the characteristics of the conditional or latent class probabilities. The latent class model is said to be *unrestricted* in exploratory latent class analysis, since researchers do not impose a priori constraints on either type of the model's parameters. In confirmatory latent class analysis, however, it is possible to investigate the correspondence between hypothesized characteristics of the latent variable and those actually exhibited by the empirically identified latent variable. In confirmatory latent class analysis, the latent class model is *restricted*—that is, researchers impose a priori size restrictions on either the conditional probabilities, the latent class probabilities, or both, depending on the specifics of the hypothesis to be tested. In the following sections we will discuss examples of both types of latent class models, along with the use and interpretation of several types of restrictions for modeling and hypothesis testing. The MLLSA program lines for the examples presented in this chapter are provided in Appendix B.

EXPLORATORY LATENT CLASS ANALYSIS

Latent class analysis is used as an exploratory method when researchers have several measures which they believe are parts of a common complex. Although the exploratory approach is typically used in the absence of an explicit theory about the specific nature of each of the latent types, it also can provide us with information concerning the adequacy of existing theory—for example, in an earlier analysis I challenged the view that Americans' tolerance for nonconformity can be best described in terms of a unidimensional continuum rather than as a set of discrete categories (McCutcheon 1985). Exploratory latent class analysis can also serve as a first step in a "stepwise" modeling procedure—such as Young (1983) proposes for examining the internal construct validity of psychiatric diagnostic criteria. In addition to political tolerance and psychiatric diagnostic criteria, the general latent class model has been used to explore a variety of topics, including racial prejudice (Tuch 1981), public attitudes toward abortion (Mooijaart 1982; Taylor 1983; McCutcheon 1986), medical diagnostic criteria (Rindskopf and Rindskopf 1986), and consumer purchasing patterns and residence satisfaction among housing assistance program participants (Dillon and Goldstein 1984).

To illustrate the use of the exploratory model, let us consider a latent classification of types of survey respondents. Four categorically scored measures from the 1982 General Social Survey[2] have been selected for this analysis: two are respondents' evaluations of surveys, and two are interviewers' evaluations of the respondents. Only white respondents will be considered in this chapter—in the final chapter we turn to a comparison of black and white respondents. The four questions we will use throughout this analysis are:

PURPOSE: In general, do you feel that surveys usually serve a good purpose, or do you feel that they are usually a waste of time and money? (Good purpose/ Depends/ Waste of time and money)

ACCURACY: How often do you think that you can trust the results of surveys? Do you think they are almost always right, right most of the time, only some of the time, or hardly ever right? (Almost always, Most of the time/ Some of the time, Hardly ever)

COOPERATION: In general, what was the respondent's attitude toward the interview? (Friendly and interested/ Cooperative but not particularly interested/ Impatient and restless/ Hostile)

UNDERSTANDING: Was the respondent's understanding of the questions good, fair, or poor? (Good/ Fair/ Poor)

These four variables net a $(3 \times 2 \times 3 \times 2)$ 36 cell crosstabulation. For notational convenience we designate the four variables as P, A, C, and U, indexed by i, j, k, l (respectively), and designate the most positive response category (the first-listed response above) as 1, with increasingly negative responses in descending order. Respondents with missing data for any of the four variables are excluded from the analysis. The resulting crosstabulation is reported in Table 3.1.

The Latent Class Probabilities

The first decision a latent class analyst must make concerns the number of latent classes (T) to identify. Although exploratory latent class analysis does not require us to have an explicit set of hypotheses to test, our analysis will proceed more smoothly if we

Table 3.1: Cross-Tabulation of Observed Variables for White Respondents: 1982 GSS

PURPOSE	ACCURACY	UNDERSTANDING	COOPERATION		
			Interested	Cooperative	Impatient, Hostile
Good	Mostly True	Good	419	35	2
		Fair, Poor	71	25	5
	Not True	Good	270	25	4
		Fair, Poor	42	16	5
Depends	Mostly True	Good	23	4	1
		Fair, Poor	6	2	0
	Not True	Good	43	9	2
		Fair, Poor	9	3	2
Waste	Mostly True	Good	26	3	0
		Fair, Poor	1	2	0
	Not True	Good	85	23	6
		Fair, Poor	13	12	8

have some general idea as to the direction we expect to go. For instance, while we may not have explicit hypotheses regarding each of the types of respondents we will identify, our previous experience may suggest that there are "ideal" respondents who believe in our research (nearly as much as we do), who understand the questions, and who are truly interested in their role as respondents. On the other hand, there also are probably some respondents who are a hair's breadth from nonparticipation—respondents who believe that surveys are worthless (or worse) and not to be trusted, who do not understand the questions, and who wish only for the interview to end. Under the assumption that there are two latent types of respondents, the degrees of freedom for the unrestricted latent class model is $(IJKL)-(I+J+K+L-3)T = 36-(3+2+3+2-3)2 = 22$. An exploratory latent class analysis of the data in Table 3.1 allows for the identification of a latent variable with up to five classes (i.e., $T = 5$).

These two classes of respondents may exhaust our initial expectations about the types of respondents described by the four measures. Next we must make an initial guess about the relative size of each of the two classes of respondents—that is, what is the proportion of "ideal" respondents (π_1^X) and what is the proportion of "skeptic" respondents (π_2^X)? We can choose to be noncommittal and initially estimate each class to be of equal size (i.e., $\pi_1^X = \pi_2^X = .5$). This decision, however, leads to increased computational costs since an increased number of iterations may be required to obtain the maximum likelihood estimates. A better approach is to note from Table 3.1 that the proportion of positive responses ranges from a low of .520 for the Accuracy variable (Mostly true are 625 of 1202) to a high of .839 for the Cooperation variable (Interested are 1008 of 1202). Consequently, we may initially estimate the proportion of ideal respondents to be closer to .65, and, recalling the requirement that the latent class probabilities sum to 1.0 (equation 2.8), we would estimate the proportion of skeptics to be .35. We would then go on to test the fit of this model to the data.

In Table 3.2 we report the decisions about the acceptability of the fit among several latent class models and the observed data. Although the Pearson chi-square (χ^2) is reported for these tests, the likelihood ratio chi-square $(L^2 = 2\sum_{ijkl} \hat{F}_{ijkl} ln[\hat{F}_{ijkl}/F_{ijkl}])$ will be the preferred test statistic because it is possible to partition the L^2. The ability to partition the L^2 means that once we have determined the number of classes (T) in the latent variable (X), hypotheses about the values of the conditional probabilities and latent class probabilities can be efficiently tested. This ability to test hypotheses is especially important for the confirmatory approach which we will examine later. Also, it should be noted that the decision criterion is set at the $p > .05$ alpha level, which follows the standard practice for statistical modelling.

The first model reported in Table 3.2, the complete independence model, is equivalent to testing a latent class model with only a single latent class $(T = 1)$ within which all of the observed variables are (locally) independent. If this model is acceptable at the .05 alpha level, we would conclude that the observed variables are not interrelated, and thus no latent variable is needed since there is no relationship between the manifest variables that requires explanation. As can be seen from Table 3.2, however, we must reject the complete independence model for these data $(L^2 = 257.26, \chi^2 = 368.67, 35df)$. The next hypothesis tests the model that there are two classes of respondents, the ideal and the skeptics, as described above. Although the two-class model appears to provide a much better fit $(L^2 = 79.34, \chi^2 = 93.26, 22df)$ than the one-class, complete independence model, we must also reject the two-class model at the .05 alpha level. Finally, we see that the three-class model provides an acceptable fit of the observed data $(L^2 = 21.93, \chi^2 = 23.59, 16df)$.

We need to note an important point with regard to the degrees of freedom in Table 3.2—although this exploratory model assumes that adding an additional class requires estimating one additional parameter for the additional latent class probability, and six additional parameters for the conditional probabilities of the additional latent class $([3-1]+[2-1]+[3-1]+[2-1])$, Table 3.2 indicates that there is a loss of only 6, not 7, degrees of freedom between the two- and three-class models. This occurs because of a special instance in which one of the conditional probabilities is found to equal zero. In such circumstances it is customary to reclaim this degree of freedom for testing the model (Clogg 1981). This parameter will be discussed more fully below.

Table 3.2: Exploratory Latent Class Models of White Respondent Types

Model	L^2	χ^2	Degrees of Freedom	Decision at .05 Alpha Level
Complete Independence	257.26	368.67	35	reject
Two-class Model	79.34	93.26	22	reject
Three-class Model	21.93	23.59	16	accept

As the data in Table 3.2 indicate, we can end our exploratory analysis at three classes, or types, of respondents. Clearly, we were incorrect in our initial hunch that all respondents could be classified as either ideal or skeptics—there must be another type as well. The latent class probabilities are the proportions of the population that are associated with each of the three classes, and these must sum to 1.00 (equation 2.8), indicating that in addition to being mutually exclusive, the classes are exhaustive. We can see, then, that the latent class probabilities tell us two important pieces of information: how many classes there are, and what proportion of the population is located in each class. (Since the conditional probabilities help us interpret the type described by each of the classes, they are usually considered before we consider the relative proportion in each of the classes.) We will see later that in the example of the three classes of respondents, about three of five (.6222) are of type I, while about one of five respondents is of each type II and type III (.2060 and .1718, respectively). These estimates of the three latent class probabilities are fairly close to the start values of .56, .22, and .22 (the program lines for this problem are reported in Appendix B).

The Latent Conditional Probabilities

The conditional probabilities represent a measure of the degree of association between each of the observed variables and each of the latent classes. Analogous to factor loadings—which represent the correlation between each of the observed variables and each of the factors—the conditional probabilities indicate the probability that an observation (individual) in a latent class will score a particular way on an observed measure. Consequently, the conditional probabilities from exploratory latent class analyses enable the analyst to interpret the nature of the classes of the latent variable.

For this reason, the conditional probabilities and latent class probabilities for the analysis of respondent types are presented in Table 3.3. What are the characteristics of the three classes of respondents identified in the analysis? The first class (I) corresponds most closely to our anticipated ideal respondents—nearly 9 of 10 (.888) in this class believed that surveys "usually serve a good purpose," 3 of 5 (.613) expressed a belief that surveys are either "almost always right" or "right most of the time," 19 of 20 (.943) were evaluated by the interviewer as "friendly and interested" during the interview, and nearly all (.998) were evaluated by the interviewer as having a good understanding of the survey questions. The third class of respondents (III) correspond most closely to the skeptics—nearly 2 of 3 (.634) believe that surveys are "a waste of time and money," 29 of 30 (.970) expressed a belief that surveys can be trusted "only some of the time" or "hardly ever," and although 3 of 4 (.753) were evaluated as having "good" understanding and nearly 2 of 3 (.641) were evaluated as friendly and interested, 1 of 10 (.103) was evaluated as either impatient and restless or hostile during the interview. The second class of respondents (II) we have characterized as "believers" because their expressed beliefs about the Purpose and Accuracy of surveys were similar to those expressed by the ideal respondents, and 7 of 10 (.688) were evaluated as being friendly and interested during the interview, but 7 of 10 (.686) were evaluated as having only fair or poor understanding of the survey questions.

A special instance arises in the estimation of this three-class model. As we see from Table 3.3, the conditional probability of an interviewer evaluating an ideal respondent as either impatient and restless or hostile is estimated to be .000. This is an example of the special case that was mentioned earlier in the discussion of the model degrees of freedom reported in Table 3.2. When a conditional probability is estimated as being .000, it is customary to reclaim the degree of freedom associated with that parameter for the model L^2 test. Since the conditional probabilities for each of the observed variables must sum to 1.00 within each of the latent classes (equation 2.12), we can see that there are 6 degrees of freedom required to estimate the conditional probabilities for skeptics,

Table 3.3: Conditional Probabilities and Latent Class Probabilities for the
Three Classes of White Respondents: 1982 GSS

Manifest Variables		Ideal (I)	Believers (II)	Skeptics (III)
			Respondent Type	
PURPOSE	Good	.888	.910	.142
	Depends	.053	.072	.225
	Waste	.059	.017	.634
ACCURACY	Mostly True	.613	.648	.030
	Not True	.387	.352	.970
COOPERATION	Interested	.943	.688	.641
	Cooperative	.057	.257	.256
	Impatient, Hostile	.000*	.055	.103
UNDERSTANDING	Good	.998	.315	.753
	Fair, Poor	.002	.686	.247
Latent Class Probabilities		.6222	.2060	.1718

* Estimated as .000 by maximum likelihood procedure.

6 for the believers, and 5 for the ideal respondents. Two additional degrees of freedom are required to estimate the latent class probabilities—recalling the requirement that these, too, must sum to 1.00 (equation 2.8). Thus 19 degrees of freedom are required to estimate the 19 unique parameters for this three-class model, leaving $(35 - 19 =)$ 16 degrees of freedom for the test of the model.

The Assignment of Observations to the Latent Classes

Frequently, latent class analysis is only a first step in the research—after defining the latent classes, the analyst may wish to assign respondents to the appropriate latent class for further analysis (see, e.g., McCutcheon 1985). Since respondents with identical scores on the observed measures are considered to be in the same latent class, the assignment to latent classes is carried out on a cell by cell basis from the crosstabulation of the observed variables. By substituting equation 2.10 into equation 2.11, we obtain the probability that respondents in cell ijk are at level t of the latent variable($P[X = t|ABC]$).

$$\pi_{ijkt}^{ABC\bar{X}} = \pi_{ijkt}^{ABCX} \Big/ \sum_t \pi_{ijkt}^{ABCX} \qquad (3.1)$$

Equation 3.1 allows us to calculate the differential contribution of each the three latent classes to each of the cells of the observed contingency table and allows us to assign the observations in a cell to the latent class with the largest conditional probability $\pi_{ijkt}^{ABC\bar{X}}$. As an example, we can calculate the probability of being in each of the 3 latent classes for the 43 respondents who are scored in cell $(2,2,1,1)$ of the crosstabulation. Using equation 2.7 we first calculate the probabilities π_{2211t}^{PACUX} for each of the latent classes.

$$\pi_{21}^{\bar{P}X}\pi_{21}^{\bar{A}X}\pi_{11}^{\bar{C}X}\pi_{11}^{\bar{U}X}\pi_{1}^{X} = .053 \times .387 \times .943 \times .998 \times .6222 = .0120$$

$$\pi_{22}^{\bar{P}X}\pi_{22}^{\bar{A}X}\pi_{12}^{\bar{C}X}\pi_{12}^{\bar{U}X}\pi_{2}^{X} = .072 \times .352 \times .688 \times .315 \times .2060 = .0013$$

$$\pi_{23}^{\bar{P}X}\pi_{23}^{\bar{A}X}\pi_{13}^{\bar{C}X}\pi_{13}^{\bar{U}X}\pi_{3}^{X} = .225 \times .970 \times .641 \times .753 \times .1718 = .0181$$

Using these estimates, we calculate the conditional probabilities for assigning the observations in cell $(2,2,1,1)$ to each of the three classes.

$$\pi_{22111}^{PACU\bar{X}} = \frac{.0120}{(.0120 + .0013 + .0181)} = .3822$$

$$\pi_{22112}^{PACU\bar{X}} = \frac{.0013}{(.0120 + .0013 + .0181)} = .0417$$

$$\pi_{22113}^{PACU\bar{X}} = \frac{.0181}{(.0120 + .0013 + .0181)} = .5761$$

Here we see that the observations in cell $(2,2,1,1)$ would be assigned to the third latent class, the skeptics, due to the higher (modal) probability for assignment to class 3 (.5761) than to either class 1 (.3822) or class 2 (.0417). Fortunately, the MLLSA program will calculate the modal probability and make the cell assignments to the latent classes.

As is clear from this example, the assignment of observations to latent classes is probabilistic—those in cell $(2,2,1,1)$ are assigned to latent class 3 because of the modal probability. This implies, however, that some error will be involved in this procedure. Clogg (1979, 1981) has developed two measures that allow us to estimate the error resulting from assigning observations to latent classes: the percent correctly classified and the lambda (λ) of the assignment. The percent correctly classified is calculated as:

$$100 \times \sum_{ijk} (\pi_{ijkt^*}^{ABC\bar{X}} \times P_{ijk})$$

where $\pi_{ijkt^*}^{ABC\bar{X}}$ is the modal probability for the cell and P_{ijk} is the proportion of the population in the cell. The lambda (Goodman and Kruskal 1954) is calculated as:

$$\lambda = \frac{E_1 - E_2}{E_1}$$

where $E_1 = 1 - \pi_{t'}^X$ which is the error rate that would result from assigning *all* observations to the largest (modal) latent class. In the earlier example, the error rate from assigning all respondents to the ideal class would be computed as: $1 - .6222 = .3778$. E_2 is the expected error rate that occurs from using the modal probabilities for the individual cells:

$$E_2 = \sum_{ijk} (1 - \pi_{ijkt^*}^{ABC\bar{X}}) P_{ijk}$$

Lambda is a measure of the closeness of association between the latent variable (X) and the joint variable (ABC). This measure can be used to supplement the L^2 to determine the improvement achieved by introducing the latent variable to account for the relationships among the observed variables.

CONFIRMATORY LATENT CLASS ANALYSIS

The exploratory latent class analysis of respondent types imposes no restrictions on the values that the conditional or latent class probabilities could take and is referred to as an *unrestricted* latent class model. We might, however, wish to test specific hypotheses regarding the values of either the conditional or latent class probabilities. For instance, we might wish to test the hypothesis that ideal respondents and believers are similar in their evaluations of surveys but are evaluated by interviewers as being dissimilar in their Understanding and Cooperation. This hypothesis requires that the analyst impose *restrictions* on the estimates of

38

the conditional probabilities (i.e., $\pi_{i1}^{\bar{P}X} = \pi_{i2}^{\bar{P}X}$ and $\pi_{j1}^{\bar{A}X} = \pi_{j2}^{\bar{A}X}$).
Analysis of restricted latent class models is referred to as *confirmatory* latent class analysis.

Confirmatory latent class analysis provides researchers with a powerful method for testing hypotheses regarding the nature of the latent variable(s). The latent class and conditional probabilities can be restricted in a variety of ways to test different types of hypotheses. As will be noted throughout the following discussion, however, restricting the latent class model requires that researchers take care to observe the effects of the restrictions being imposed on the model, so that the latent class and conditional probabilities continue to meet the requirement of summing to 1.0 (equations 2.8 and 2.12), and no cell is defined as having an expected probability of 0.0 for *all* classes of the latent variable (equation 2.16).

In general, there are two types of restrictions, or constraints, that can be placed on each of the two types of parameters: equality constraints and specific value constraints. Equality constraints require that two or more of either the modeled latent class probabilities or conditional probabilities take on the same value—in the instance of equal latent class probabilities, this constraint tests the hypothesis that the classes are of equal size; in the instance of equal conditional probabilities, the constraint tests the hypothesis that observations in two or more classes are equally likely to be found at a given level of an observed variable. Specific value constraints, on the other hand, require that one or more of either the modeled latent class or conditional probabilities equal a value that has an a priori specification. Nearly all of the remaining latent class models that we consider will have some restrictions imposed on them. In this section we will examine the use and interpretation of restrictions on conditional and latent class probabilities.

Conditional Probability Restrictions

Frequently, researchers wish to place a priori constraints on the conditional probabilities in order to test hypotheses regarding the nature of the contributions of the observed measures to the latent classes. For instance, in our example of respondent types, we might be interested in testing the hypothesis that *all* ideal respondents have "Good" Understanding or the hypothesis that believers and ideal respondents evaluate the Accuracy and Purpose of surveys similarly but are evaluated differently on their Understanding and Cooperation. Each of these hypotheses represents a different type of constraint on the conditional probabilities and consequently results in different types of interpretations.

Specific value constraints restrict the maximum likelihood procedure to fitting a latent class model in which one or more of the conditional probabilities has been set to a specified value. This is usually done when the researcher's theory requires a specific value. We could, for instance, specify that the conditional probability of a particular response (for one of the latent classes) equals .5. This would test the hypothesis that respondents in that class have a 50/50 probability of giving that particular response. Or, we could test the hypothesis that in one of the classes, the responses to a particular question mirror those found in the total population. This would be accomplished by restricting the conditional probabilities for that variable to the probabilities calculated for the entire population.

Perhaps the most useful type of specific value constraint, however, is the restriction of conditional probabilities to be either 1.0 or 0.0. In our present example, we test the hypothesis that all skeptics are truly skeptical of the Accuracy of surveys—that is, that respondents classified as skeptics *always* choose "Not True" to the Accuracy question. This is equivalent to setting the restriction that $\pi_{23}^{\bar{A}X} = 1.0$, and, because of equation 2.9, $\pi_{13}^{\bar{A}X} = 0.0$. We also test the hypothesis that *all* ideal respondents have a "Good" Understanding of the survey questions: that $\pi_{11}^{\bar{U}X} = 1.0$, and that $\pi_{21}^{\bar{U}X} = 0.0$. Finally, since the exploratory approach found that no ideal respondent was "Impatient or Hostile," we add this as an exact indicator restriction ($\pi_{13}^{\bar{C}X} = 0.0$), noting that the ideal respondents' conditional probabilities for the other two Cooperation responses ($\pi_{11}^{\bar{C}X}$ and $\pi_{12}^{\bar{C}X}$) remain unrestricted. The fit of the model with these restrictions is reported in Table 3.4.

As we see in Table 3.4, the addition of the specific value and equality restrictions increases the L^2 of the three-class model. Since these three models are hierarchical (or nested), we can partition the L^2 to check for the acceptability of model restrictions by differenc-

Table 3.4: Confirmatory Latent Class Models of White
Respondent Types

Model	L^2	χ^2	Degrees of Freedom
Unrestricted Three-class Model	21.93	23.59	16
Specific Value Restrictions*	22.13	24.45	18
Specific Value and Equality Restrictions*	25.59	27.01	21

* See text for description of restrictions.

ing respective model L^2's. For example, to test the acceptability
of the specific value restrictions, we subtract the L^2 (and degrees
of freedom) of the unrestricted model (21.93) from the L^2 (and
degrees of freedom) of the restricted model (22.13) which results
in an acceptable increase in the L^2 (0.20, with $18 - 16 = 2df$). We
conclude that the fit is acceptable if the increase in the L^2 is small
relative to its degrees of freedom—if, instead, the increase in the L^2
nets a probability that is less than .05, then the additional model
restrictions cause the model to differ significantly from the data.
Since restricting these parameters leads to an L^2 increase of only
0.20, and reduces by 2 the number of estimated model parameters,
we conclude that the restrictions substantially improve the fit of
the model.

When imposing specific value restrictions, the researcher must
take care not to define a latent class model which disallows combinations observed in the data. For instance, in the restricted model
outlined above, the skeptics class is restricted from including any
respondents who evaluate the Accuracy of surveys as Mostly True.
If we also imposed specific value restrictions to disallow the ideal
and believer classes from evaluating the Purpose of surveys as a
Waste of Time and Money, the model would completely exclude
respondents who evaluate the Accuracy of surveys as Mostly True
and evaluate the Purpose of surveys as a Waste—even though Table 3.1 shows there are 32 such respondents. When this type of
error occurs, the L^2 may take on a negative value, and the modal

conditional probability for the affected cells of the crosstabulation will be 0.0.

Unlike specific value restrictions, equality restrictions do not require an a priori specification of a value for the conditional probabilities. Instead, two or more of the conditional probability estimates are restricted to equaling one another, such as when the conditional probability of an observed measure is restricted to be identical for two or more classes. This restriction tests the hypothesis that the observed variable does not discriminate between (or among) the specified classes. Care must be taken not to impose this type of equality restriction on *all* of the conditional probabilities for two (or more) classes from the same population, since this would be equivalent to testing the hypothesis that the two classes are *identical*—implying that there is only one class, not two.

Restricting the conditional probability of each level of a measure to equal each of the other levels of the variable tests the hypothesis that respondents in the class are as likely to give one response as another to the question. This type of equality restriction will not be considered here because it is the same as an exact indicator restriction—for a dichotomous measure this restriction is the same as restricting each conditional probability to equal .50, for trichotomies the restrictions equal .333, and so forth. As with exact indicator restrictions, caution must be taken to ensure that conditional probabilities for each variable sum to 1.0 within each of the latent classes.

In the final model reported in Table 3.4, equality restrictions have been imposed on the ideal respondents' and believer respondents' evaluations of surveys. These restrictions test the general hypothesis that these two types of respondents differ only with respect to their Understanding of the survey questions and their level of Cooperation during the interview. Specifically, we will impose the equality restrictions that members of these two classes are equally likely to believe the Accuracy of surveys are True $(\pi_{11}^{\bar{A}X} = \pi_{12}^{\bar{A}X})$ and equally likely to believe that the Purpose of surveys is Good $(\pi_{11}^{\bar{P}X} = \pi_{12}^{\bar{P}X})$ and Depends $(\pi_{21}^{\bar{P}X} = \pi_{22}^{\bar{P}X})$.

The data reported in Table 3.4 indicate that the addition of these three conditional probability equality restrictions net an acceptable increase in the L^2 of $(25.59 - 22.13 =)$ 3.46 with $(21 - 18 =)$ 3 degrees of freedom, thus supporting the hypothesis that believers and ideal respondents hold similar subjective dispositions toward surveys. Caution must be observed when imposing several restrictions in one step, however, since it is possible to obtain an apparently acceptable L^2 that masks an unacceptable restriction. Consequently, when the increase in an L^2 with several degrees of freedom exceeds the .05 level for a single degree of freedom, it is advisable to test each of the restrictions separately.

The conditional probability estimates for the restricted latent class model of respondent types are reported in Table 3.5. These estimates differ only slightly from the exploratory results reported in Table 3.3, even though we have tested several hypotheses regarding the respondent types: no ideal respondent was evaluated as Impatient or Hostile; the Understanding of all ideal respondents was evaluated as Good; no skeptics evaluated the Accuracy of surveys as Mostly True, and the believers and ideal respondents differ only on their Understanding and Cooperation, not on their subjective evaluations of surveys. Finally, we note that over 3 of 5 of the respondents can be classified as ideal (.6190), more than 1 of 5 can be classified as believers (.2232), and about 1 of 6 can be classified as skeptics (.1579).

Latent Class Probability Restrictions

In a sense, the specification of the number of latent classes (T) is a restriction placed on the latent class model. Typically, however, this specification is not regarded as a restriction. Instead, the notion of restrictions on the latent class probabilities mirror the types of restrictions found for the conditional probabilities. That is, specific value restrictions on the latent class probabilities specify a priori values for one or more of the latent classes, and equality restrictions on the latent class probabilities restrict two or more of the classes to be of equal size.

In practice, specific value restrictions on the latent class probabilities may have somewhat limited application in social research. Researchers may, for example, test the hypothesis that a given class accounts for a specific proportion of the population. The procedure

Table 3.5: Conditional Probabilities and Latent Class Probabilities for the
Three Restricted Classes of White Respondents: 1982 GSS

Manifest Variables		Respondent Type		
		Ideal (I)	Believers (II)	Skeptics (III)
PURPOSE	Good	.887†	.887†	.110
	Depends	.060†	.060†	.228
	Waste	.053	.053	.661
ACCURACY	Mostly True	.617†	.617†	.000*
	Not True	.383	.383	1.000
COOPERATION	Interested	.943	.683	.649
	Cooperative	.057	.260	.248
	Impatient, Hostile	.000*	.058	.103
UNDERSTANDING	Good	1.000*	.338	.765
	Fair, Poor	.000	.662	.235
Latent Class Probabilities		.6190	.2232	.1579

†Equality restriction imposed.
*Exact indicator restriction imposed.

for partitioning the L^2 when restricting the latent class probabilities is similar to that of partitioning the L^2 when restricting the conditional probabilities—one degree of freedom is freed for each restricted latent class probability, and these degrees of freedom are used to test the acceptability of the fit between the model with the restrictions and the model without the restrictions. Since the latent class probabilities must sum to 1.0 (equation 2.8), no more than $T-1$ latent class probabilities can be restricted, and care must be taken to specify values that satisfy this summing to 1.0. Unlike the use of this type of restriction for conditional probabilities, however, we would not test the hypothesis that all of the population is in a given class (i.e., $\pi_t^X = 1.0$), or the hypothesis that none of the population is in a given class (i.e., $\pi_t^X = 0.0$), since the former case is actually the independence model, and the latter is handled by testing the fit of a model with one fewer classes in the latent variable.

Equality restrictions on the latent class probabilities are somewhat more useful constraints for latent class modeling. Researchers can, for instance, test the hypothesis that two or more classes in the population are of equal size. Only one degree of freedom is required to estimate latent class probabilities that are constrained to be equal; thus, if two are restricted to be equal, one degree of freedom is freed, if three are restricted, two degrees of freedom are freed, and so forth. Since the latent class probabilities must sum to 1.0 (equation 2.8), equality constraints can be imposed on no more than $T - 1$ of the latent class probabilities. If the partitioned increase in the L^2 is acceptably low (i.e., nonsignificant), we can accept the hypothesis that the two or more classes are of equal size. This type of constraint is particularly useful when comparing the latent classes of two or more populations—a topic we take up in Chapter 5.

Occasionally, researchers may wish to test the hypothesis that all of the latent classes are of equal size—that the latent classes are equiprobable (i.e., $\pi_1^X = \pi_2^X = \cdots = \pi_T^X$). In such an instance, equality constraints will not work, because equality restrictions can be imposed on only $T - 1$ of the latent class probabilities, which means that the unrestricted class need not take on the same value as the other classes. Consequently, the analyst should use specific value constraints in which the restricted latent class probabilities are specified to equal the necessary value, leaving the unrestricted class only one possible value due to the requirement that they sum to 1.0. For instance, to test the hypothesis that the three respondent types were equiprobable, each of the first two classes must be restricted to equal .333, leaving the final class to equal .334.

Although a detailed example of restrictions on the latent class probabilities is not presented here, we will consider use of these types of restrictions when comparing the latent respondent types of whites and blacks in the fifth chapter. The program lines presented in Tables 3.3 and 3.5 are reported in Appendix B.

4. ANALYZING SCALE RESPONSE PATTERNS

In this chapter we will examine a special use of restricted latent class models to analyze the scalability of a set of observed responses. This approach assumes that the classes of the latent variable represent a sequence of levels of "difficulty" for an underlying trait; that the observed measures can be rank ordered in terms of their difficulty on the latent variable (X). Consequently, respondents in progressively higher classes of the latent variable are likely to have scored "correctly" on the progressively more difficult measures, while those in the lower latent classes are likely to have scored "incorrectly" even on the "easier" measures. Torgerson (1958) has discussed this use of the latent structure model as a probability analogue of the Guttman scale.

Guttman scaling assumes that a set of dichotomously coded observed measures can be ordered according to their difficulty to construct a unidimensional scale of an underlying phenomenon. Although Guttman scaling has an intuitive appeal, it has been frequently criticized for its deterministic form and the ad hoc nature of the evaluation criteria for the scale. The deterministic form of Guttman scaling is especially evident in assumptions concerning error rates—it requires the dubious assumption that each of the measures is error free. Further, the scale evaluation criteria— the coefficient of reproducibility and coefficient of scalability—are based on "rules of thumb" which have little statistical justification.

In this chapter we examine several probabilistic approaches to scalogram analysis which incorporate notions of measurement error, and which provide evaluation criteria that are based on probabilistic ideas. To illustrate our discussion, we will analyze four political campaign participation items drawn from the 1980 National Election Study (NES)[3] that measures respondents' level of participation in 1980 political campaigns. Researchers wishing to conduct a complete analysis of the scalability of a set of survey items should consult Clogg and Sawyer's (1981) comprehensive discussion.

In the postelection survey, the NES respondents were asked about their political participation during the 1980 campaigns. In the analysis of this section we will focus on four types of campaign activities:

V: In talking to a lot of people about elections, we often find that a lot of people were not able to vote because (they weren't old enough) they weren't registered, they were sick, or they just didn't have the time. How about you, did you vote in the elections this November?

I: During the campaign, did you talk to any people and try to show them why they should vote for one of the parties or candidates?

A: Did you go to any political meetings, rallies, fund-raising dinners, or things like that?

W: Did you do any work for one of the parties or candidates (during the campaign)?

To facilitate the analysis, only respondents who answered either yes or no to each of the four campaign participation items are included in this analysis. This results in a reduction from 1408 respondents in the total postelection 1980 NES sample to 1402 respondents for this analysis. The crosstabulation of these four items is presented in Table 4.1.

Although there are $k!$ (24) *possible* orderings of a set of k items, Guttman scaling assumes that there is only one correct ordering of items from least difficult to most difficult. Moreover, the logic of Guttman scaling suggests that, within the single ordering, once a person responds negatively to an easier item, he or she will respond negatively to each of the remaining items. Thus the first order of business is to determine the rank ordering of items by difficulty. One possible approach to determining the proper ordering of items is to refer either to theory or previous research. The approach we shall use is to determine the difficulty of an item by inspecting the marginal distribution of affirmative answers for each of the four items. These are reported in Table 4.2.

The data presented in Table 4.2 indicate that it was least difficult for respondents to vote (71.5%), most difficult for them to have worked for a candidate or party (3.6%), and that influencing others and attending meetings or rallies are intermediate to the Vote and Work items. Thus the data in Table 4.2 suggest ordering the four campaign activity items as (V, I, A, W), where voting (V) is the least difficult (i.e., most readily participated in) item, and working for a candidate or party (W) is the most difficult (i.e., least readily participated in) item. If we designate an affirmative response as 1 and a negative response as 2, there are $k+1$ response patterns that are considered correct for the four forms of campaign participation:

(1,1,1,1)   (1,1,1,2)   (1,1,2,2)   (1,2,2,2)   (2,2,2,2)

Since all of the items are dichotomous, there are $2^k = 2^4 = 16$ possible response patterns for the difficulty ordering of the four

Table 4.1: Cross-tabulation of Four Political Campaign
Participation Items: 1980 NES

| | | | VOTE | |
			Yes	No
WORK	ATTEND	INFLUENCE		
Yes	Yes	Yes	27	0
		No	2	0
	No	Yes	16	0
		No	4	1
No	Yes	Yes	40	3
		No	32	2
	No	Yes	339	83
		No	543	310

Table 4.2: Marginal Distribution of Responses to Four
Campaign Participation Items (N=1402): 1980 NES

Participation Item*	Yes	No
Vote	1003	399
	71.5%	28.5%
Influence	508	894
	36.2%	63.8%
Attend	106	1296
	7.6%	92.4%
Work	50	1352
	3.6%	96.4%

* See text for full description of items.

forms of participation. Consequently, $(16 - 5 =)$ 11 of these patterns are incorrect. The distribution of the 5 correct response types are reported in Table 4.3.

We can estimate the error rate per response for these data by dividing the sum of yes responses where no responses were expected and no responses where yes responses were expected by the total number of responses. This error rate, which we denote as e_2, is calculated as:

$$e_2 = E_2/(kn)$$

Table 4.3: Distribution of 1980 NES Respondents in Scale Types Corresponding to Ordering (V,I,A,W)

Scale Type	Response Pattern	Frequency	Percentage
1	(1,1,1,1)	27	1.93
2	(1,1,1,2)	40	2.85
3	(1,1,2,2)	339	24.18
4	(1,2,2,2)	543	38.73
5	(2,2,2,2)	310	22.11
Total in scale types		1259	89.80
Errors		143	10.20
Total		1402	100.00

where E_2 is the sum of incorrect responses, k is the number of items in the scale, and n is the number of respondents. We find that $E_2 = 151$, so $e_2 = 151/(4 \times 1402) = .027$. Guttman's *coefficient of reproducibility* is calculated as $1 - e_2 = 1 - .027 = .973$, well above the commonly accepted minimum of 0.9 for concluding that the items represent a valid scale. As Clogg and Sawyer (1981) note, it is common practice to calculate the minimum amount of reproducibility in a set of items that could be obtained by knowledge of the marginal distributions alone. To do this, we first calculate the maximum error rate by summing the item-specific marginal minimums (Table 4.2), and divide that sum by the total number of responses:

$$e_1 = E_1/(kn)$$

With the four campaign activity items we find that the maximum number of response errors is 1063, so $e_1 = 1063/(4 \times 1402) = .190$. Thus, we can estimate the *minimum marginal reproducibility* for this sample as $1 - e_1 = 1 - .190 = .810$.

The final measure usually associated with Guttman scales is Guttman's *coefficient of scalability*, which estimates the proportional reduction in error rates

$$S = (e_1 - e_2)/e_1$$

and is .858 for the four 1980 NES campaign activity items. This estimate well exceeds the commonly accepted minimum of 0.6 for concluding that the items are unidimensional and cumulative.

MODELS WITH ERRORS OF MEASUREMENT

The deterministic nature of Guttman scaling has led to a number of proposed alternatives that include response error as an integral part of the measurement model. These alternatives assume that each of the individual items has an associated measurement error. For example, persons who are politically very active may have been unable to vote because of illness on election day, or persons who are politically nonactive may have attended a political dinner with a friend. Consequently, none of the items is believed to be a perfect measure—responses to each of the measured items are probabilistic. As we will see, all of the models considered in this section can be expressed as special instances of the restricted latent class model we examined in the previous chapter.

Proctor's Model

The first probabilistic variation on the Guttman model we consider is the model proposed by Proctor (1970) in which each of the scale items has error rates that are assumed to be homogeneous over all items and scale types. The Proctor model can be viewed as a special case of the latent class model in which one each of $k+1$ latent classes represents each of the 1 to $k + 1$ scale positions. For example, if the error rate of the items equals .05 (a 5% probability of giving an incorrect answer), a person located at position 3 (i.e., 1,1,2,2) on the four-item latent scale of campaign activity has a .95 probability of answering each of the two easier items affirmatively and a .05 probability of answering the two more difficult questions affirmatively. Whereas the Guttman model assumes that all persons at position 3 will answer affirmatively to the two easier items and negatively to the two more difficult items, the Proctor model assumes that the responses to the scale items are subject to error. Consequently, to obtain the Proctor model, equality constraints are imposed on the conditional probabilities of the scale items for each of the five scale positions (latent classes)—*all* of the conditional probabilities are constrained to equal the same value.

$$\pi_{11}^{\bar{V}X} = \pi_{11}^{\bar{I}X} = \pi_{11}^{\bar{A}X} = \pi_{11}^{\bar{W}X}$$
$$= \pi_{12}^{\bar{V}X} = \pi_{12}^{\bar{I}X} = \pi_{12}^{\bar{A}X} = \pi_{22}^{\bar{W}X}$$

$$= \pi_{13}^{\bar{V}X} = \pi_{13}^{IX} = \pi_{23}^{\bar{A}X} = \pi_{23}^{\bar{W}X} \qquad (4.1)$$

$$= \pi_{14}^{\bar{V}X} = \pi_{24}^{IX} = \pi_{24}^{\bar{A}X} = \pi_{24}^{\bar{W}X}$$

$$= \pi_{25}^{\bar{V}X} = \pi_{25}^{IX} = \pi_{25}^{\bar{A}X} = \pi_{25}^{\bar{W}X}$$

The estimation of the Proctor model requires only 1 degree of freedom for the conditional probability estimate and k degrees of freedom to estimate the latent class probabilities for the $k + 1$ scale positions, or types. As we see in Table 4.4, the Proctor model fails to provide an adequate fit for the four item campaign activity scale $(L^2 = 138.19, 10df)$. As Clogg and Sawyer (1981, 253) note, there are several reasons why the Proctor model might fail to fit the data: (1) the items may be ordered incorrectly, (2) the items may not represent a single underlying dimension, (3) the response error rates may not be truly equal—they may vary by item or latent scale type (latent class) or both, (4) there may be a subpopulation in which the item ordering is completely different from that hypothesized, or (5) a combination of these factors.

Although we must reject Proctor's model for the four-item campaign activity scale, we should note that the error rate (conditional probability) was estimated to be .046, and that the proportions of the population estimated in the five scale types (latent class probabilities) were

.0201	.0190	.2920	.4260	.2429

respectively. Since this model assumes response error rates, the estimated proportion of the population in a scale type need not equal the observed proportion in the scale type. Thus, while .0193 of the cases were observed in scale type 1 (Table 4.3), Proctor's model estimates that .0201 of the population were in this highly active class in the 1980 political campaigns.

Item-specific Error Rate Model

The second model we examine—the Item-specific error rate model—relaxes Proctor's assumption that all of the scale items

Table 4.4: L^2 and χ^2 Values for Scale Models Involving
Response Error Rates

Model	DF	L^2	χ^2
Proctor's model	10	138.19	137.27
Item-specific error rates	7	36.63	36.77
True-type-specific error rates	7*	89.02	86.54
Lazarsfeld's latent distance model	5	14.79	12.38

*One error rate estimated as 0.0.

have the same error rates (Clogg and Sawyer 1981). Instead, the Item-specific error rate model assumes that there is a specific response error rate that is associated with each of the k items. Like the Proctor model, the Item-specific error rate model is a special case of the restricted latent class model. Now, however, the error rates (conditional probabilities) are restricted such that:

$$
\begin{aligned}
\pi_{11}^{\bar{V}X} &= \pi_{12}^{\bar{V}X} = \pi_{13}^{\bar{V}X} = \pi_{14}^{\bar{V}X} = \pi_{25}^{\bar{V}X}, \\
\pi_{11}^{\bar{I}X} &= \pi_{12}^{\bar{I}X} = \pi_{13}^{\bar{I}X} = \pi_{24}^{\bar{I}X} = \pi_{25}^{\bar{I}X}, \\
\pi_{11}^{\bar{A}X} &= \pi_{12}^{\bar{A}X} = \pi_{23}^{\bar{A}X} = \pi_{24}^{\bar{A}X} = \pi_{25}^{\bar{A}X}, \\
\pi_{11}^{\bar{W}X} &= \pi_{22}^{\bar{W}X} = \pi_{23}^{\bar{W}X} = \pi_{24}^{\bar{W}X} = \pi_{25}^{\bar{W}X}.
\end{aligned}
\tag{4.2}
$$

Since we are estimating error rates (conditional probabilities) for each of the k items with this model, we use k degrees of freedom for these estimates. We also use an additional k degrees of freedom to estimate the proportion of the population in each of the $k+1$ scale types (latent classes). Thus the Item-specific error rate model estimates $2k$ parameters.

Compared to the Proctor model, it is clear that the Item-specific error rate model provides a substantial improvement of fit to the observed data. The Proctor model and Item-specific error rate model are hierarchical, so we can partition the L^2 to test the improvement of fit obtained by estimating the item-specific error rates. When we partition the L^2's reported in Table 4.4, it becomes clear that the Item-specific error rate model nets an improvement of fit over the Proctor model ($L^2 = 138.19 - 36.63 = 101.56, df = 10 - 7 = 3$). The error rates estimated by this model for the four campaign activity items indicate that voting is least subject to error (.003), that attempting to influence another person is most subject to error (.211), and that working for a candidate or party and attending a meeting or rally have intermediate response error rates (.015 and .025, respectively). Also, the proportion of the population estimated to be in each of the five scale types is (respectively):

.0216 .0333 .2043 .4576 .2832

The model L^2 reported in Table 4.4, however, indicates that the Item-specific error rate model ($36.63, 7df$) does not provide an adequate fit to the data—we must also reject this model. Consequently, we must reject the model which assumes that the response errors for each of the four campaign activity scale items is constant over each of the scale types.

True-type-specific Error Rate Model

The third type of model we consider—the True-type-specific error rate model—relaxes the Proctor model assumption that the error rate is homogeneous with regard to scale type (Clogg and Sawyer 1981). Relaxing this assumption means that persons at differing locations on the latent campaign participation scale are different *types* of respondents and are subject to differing *type-specific* response error rates. We should note, however, that the True-type-specific error rate model requires the assumption that all of the campaign participation scale items are subject to the same response error rate *within* each of the types—that is, within each of the latent classes each of the items is equally likely to be incorrectly answered. As with the previous two models, the True-type-specific error rate model also can be expressed as a special case of the latent class model. We can specify this model by imposing the following restrictions:

$$\pi_{11}^{\bar{V}X} = \pi_{11}^{\bar{I}X} = \pi_{11}^{\bar{A}X} = \pi_{11}^{\bar{W}X},$$

$$\pi_{12}^{\bar{V}X} = \pi_{12}^{\bar{I}X} = \pi_{12}^{\bar{A}X} = \pi_{22}^{\bar{W}X},$$
$$\pi_{13}^{\bar{V}X} = \pi_{13}^{\bar{I}X} = \pi_{23}^{\bar{A}X} = \pi_{23}^{\bar{W}X}, \quad (4.3)$$
$$\pi_{14}^{\bar{V}X} = \pi_{24}^{\bar{I}X} = \pi_{24}^{\bar{A}X} = \pi_{24}^{\bar{W}X},$$
$$\pi_{25}^{\bar{V}X} = \pi_{25}^{\bar{I}X} = \pi_{25}^{\bar{A}X} = \pi_{25}^{\bar{W}X}.$$

Since there are $k + 1$ types (latent classes) in the model, and each type requires the estimation of a separate response error rate, $k + 1$ degrees of freedom are required to estimate the type-specific error rates. As with the previous two models, k degrees of freedom are required to estimate the proportion of the population in each of the $k + 1$ scale types (latent classes). To estimate the of the True-type-specific error rate model, then, requires estimating $2k + 1$ parameters.

The L^2 for the True-type-specific error rate (Table 4.4) shows an improvement in fit over the Proctor model. By removing the assumption that all five scale types are subject to the same response error rate, we use $(10 - 6 =)$ 4 additional degrees of freedom to obtain an improvement of fit L^2 of $(138.19 - 89.02 =)$ 49.17. This indicates that we must reject the assumption of a single response error rate that is identical for each of the scale types. Instead, there appear to be five error rates, one for each of the five scale types. The estimates of the five type-specific error rates are

.000   .175   .104   .025   .007

for each of the types 1 through 5, respectively. These estimates suggest that response error rates are highest for the intermediate types (i.e., 2 and 3) and decrease at the extremes (types 1, 4, and 5). The proportions of the population estimated to be in the five scale types are:

.0156   .0050   .3687   .3961   .2146.

These estimated scale type proportions are larger than the observed scale type proportions reported in Table 4.3, because of the assumption that the 143 "errors" in Table 4.3 are attributable to response error. A quick comparison of these data indicates that the greatest differences occur in the classes with the highest estimated response error. Like the Proctor model and the Item-specific error rate model, the L^2 reported in Table 4.4 for the True-type-specific error rate model ($89.02, 7df$) leads us to conclude that this model provides an unacceptable fit to the observed data.

Lazarsfeld's Latent Distance Model

The final type of response error rate model we consider is the *latent distance model*, which was first proposed by Lazarsfeld (1950a and 1950b) as a latent structure modeling approach to item scaling. The latent distance model is most similar to the Item-specific error rate model in that it assumes that error rates are item-specific rather than type-specific. Unlike the Item-specific error rate model, however, the latent distance model assumes that the response error rate for affirmative answers to an item differs from the response error rate for negative answers to the item. This assumption is implemented for all of the scale items other than the two most "extreme" items—that is, the easiest and most difficult items. As Lazarsfeld and Henry discuss in detail, it is not possible to estimate more than one reliable error rate for each of the two extreme scale items (1968, 123–138). Consequently, they note that it is important to be sure a priori, on the basis of the content of the two items, that they can serve as "anchors" for the scale—i.e., that one of these is the easiest of the items and the other is the most difficult. Each intermediate item, then, has two error rate estimates: one for the affirmative responses and another for the negative responses.

The latent distance model error rates can be estimated by imposing the following restrictions on the conditional probabilities:

$$\pi_{11}^{\bar{V}X} = \pi_{12}^{\bar{V}X} = \pi_{13}^{\bar{V}X} = \pi_{14}^{\bar{V}X} = \pi_{25}^{\bar{V}X}$$
$$\pi_{11}^{\bar{I}X} = \pi_{12}^{\bar{I}X} = \pi_{13}^{\bar{I}X}$$
$$\pi_{24}^{\bar{I}X} = \pi_{25}^{\bar{I}X}$$
$$\pi_{11}^{\bar{A}X} = \pi_{12}^{\bar{A}X} \tag{4.4}$$
$$\pi_{23}^{\bar{A}X} = \pi_{24}^{\bar{A}X} = \pi_{25}^{\bar{A}X}$$
$$\pi_{11}^{\bar{W}X} = \pi_{22}^{\bar{W}X} = \pi_{23}^{\bar{W}X} = \pi_{24}^{\bar{W}X} = \pi_{25}^{\bar{W}X}$$

As can be seen from these restrictions, there are two error rates (conditional probabilities) estimated for each of the intermediate scale items, and one error rate for each of the two extreme scale items. Thus the latent distance model requires estimating $2(k - 2) + 2$ or $2k - 2$ different error rates. We must also estimate the proportions of the population in each of the scale types (latent class probabilities), which add another k parameters to be estimated, resulting in a total of $3k - 2$ degrees of freedom required for estimating the latent distance model.

Partitioning the L^2's in Table 4.4 shows that the latent distance model provides a clear improvement in fit over both the Proctor model $(L^2 = 123.40, 5df)$ and the Item-specific error rate model $(L^2 = 21.84, 2df)$. An improvement of fit L^2 between the True-type-specific error rate model and the latent distance model cannot be tested by partitioning the two model L^2's, because the two models are not hierarchical (nested)—the error rates (conditional probabilities) of the True-type-specific error rate model are restricted within scale types, while the error rates of the latent distance model are restricted within scale items. The latent distance model appears to provide a better fit to the data $(L^2 = 14.79, 5df)$ than the True-type-specific model $(L^2 = 89.02, 7df)$. Since we cannot partition the L^2 to test if there is an improvement of fit of one these models over the other, however, we do not have an efficient statistical test to help us decide whether one or the other of the models provides a better description of the data.

In instances when two (or more) models provide good fits to the observed data, and neither model can be preferred on the basis of the goodness of fit criteria, Clogg and Sawyer (1981) suggest comparing the Lambdas and the "Percentage (of observations) Correctly Allocated" (see Chapter 3) of the two models as evidence for selecting one over the other. While neither of these statistics is intended as a substitute for the goodness-of-fit criteria, they may aid in a choice between models that appear equally acceptable. Thus, if we compare the Lambda and Percent Correctly Allocated of the True-type-specific error rate model (.88 and 93.0%) with those of the latent distance model (.69 and 84.0%), it appears that the True-type-specific model may be somewhat better.

The six error rate estimates and the estimated proportions of the population in each of the five scale types of the latent distance model for the four-item campaign activity scale are reported in Ta-

Table 4.5: Error Rates and Scale-Type Proportions Estimated Under
Lazarsfeld's Latent Distance Model

Intrinsic Type of Individual	Scale Type	Probability of Response Error in Answering Item				Proportion in Scale Type
		V	I	A	W	
1	(1,1,1,1)	.001	.167	.385	.002	.0335
2	(1,1,1,2)	.001	.167	.385	.002	.0488
3	(1,1,2,2)	.001	.167	.027	.002	.1558
4	(1,2,2,2)	.001	.215	.027	.002	.4774
5	(2,2,2,2)	.001	.215	.027	.002	.2844

ble 4.5. The error rates indicate that a positive response (coded 1)
to the Attend item has a much higher response error rate (.385)
than any of the other responses, while the error rate for the negative response (coded 2) for that item is a greater deal smaller
(.027), suggesting that the Attend item discriminates better for
the more active partisans than the less active partisans. More serious, perhaps, both the positive and negative response error rates
for the Influence item are quite high (.167 and .215, respectively),
thus cautioning us in the use of this item for a composite scale.
The two end items—Vote and Work—have identical error rates for
positive and negative response rates (equation 4.4), each of which
is quite small (.001 and .002, respectively), indicating that these
two items "anchor" this scale quite well. We also note that only a
little more than 3% (.0335) of the 1980 population are estimated
to comprise the most active class (scale type 1), which involves
high probabilities (.615 to .998) of participating in each of the four
campaign activities; we also note that the most active class out-
numbers the least active class (scale type 5) by over 8 to 1 (.2822).
By far the largest class, however, is that of the "voting special-
ists" (scale type 2)—respondents with a high probability of voting
(.999) but a low probability (.002 to .215) of participation in any
of the other three campaign activities. This class is estimated to
comprise nearly half (.4774) of the 1980 population.

GOODMAN'S SCALE MODEL

Each of the scale models discussed in the previous section
relaxed Guttman's deterministic assumption by introducing the

possibility of error rates associated with the scale responses. All of these models, however, retain Guttman's original assumption that all persons in a population are scalable on the same response pattern—that all deviations from the scale pattern are attributable to stochastic disturbances. Goodman (1975) proposes an alternative model in which the assumption of population homogeneity is relaxed. In this section we will briefly examine the four-item campaign activity scale using four versions of Goodman's scale model: (1) a model assuming that part of the population is *intrinsically scalable* according to the Guttman ordering of items, and that the rest of the population is *intrinsically unscalable*, (2) a model like the first, but with a Proctor model response error rate for the intrinsically scalable portion of the population, (3) a biform model in which more than one ordering of the items is assumed to occur in the population, and (4) a model like the third in which one of the items is found to be "collapsible" in the analysis—that is, one of the items is found to provide inadequate discrimination between scale types.

The first variant of the Goodman scale model assumes that some proportion of the population, denoted π_0, are intrinsically unscalable, and that the remainder of the population $(1 - \pi_0)$ is scalable according to the Guttman ordering of the scale items. The addition of the *unscalable type* to the model with $k + 1$ scale types means that there are now $k + 2$ types that need to be estimated for Goodman's scale model. This model, like those considered previously, can be expressed as a special case of the restricted latent class model in which specific value restrictions are placed on the conditional probabilities of the five scalable types, but no restrictions are placed on the conditional probabilities of the unscalable type:

$$
\begin{aligned}
1.0 &= \pi_{11}^{\bar{V}X} = \pi_{11}^{\bar{I}X} = \pi_{11}^{\bar{A}X} = \pi_{11}^{\bar{W}X}, \\
&= \pi_{12}^{\bar{V}X} = \pi_{12}^{\bar{I}X} = \pi_{12}^{\bar{A}X} = \pi_{22}^{\bar{W}X}, \\
&= \pi_{13}^{\bar{V}X} = \pi_{13}^{\bar{I}X} = \pi_{23}^{\bar{A}X} = \pi_{23}^{\bar{W}X}, \\
&= \pi_{14}^{\bar{V}X} = \pi_{24}^{\bar{I}X} = \pi_{24}^{\bar{A}X} = \pi_{24}^{\bar{W}X}, \\
&= \pi_{25}^{\bar{V}X} = \pi_{25}^{\bar{I}X} = \pi_{25}^{\bar{A}X} = \pi_{25}^{\bar{W}X}.
\end{aligned}
\tag{4.5}
$$

Table 4.6: L^2 and χ^2 Values for Goodman Scale Models

Model	DF	L^2	χ^2
Intrinsically unscalable	6	20.55	17.51
Proctor-Goodman	5	20.63	16.31
Biform scale	5	7.02	5.94
Biform scale with Type 2 excluded	6	6.77	5.62

All respondents who answer according to one of the five Guttman response patterns are included with certainty into the appropriate class; these response patterns are said to be *deterministically* restricted to a given class. Those respondents who fail to answer according to the Guttman ordering—143 NES respondents on the four campaign activity items (Table 4.3)—are included in the remaining class, which is the unscalable type. Consequently, in this variant of the Goodman scale model we assume local independence among the scale items for the unscalable type—respondents who do not respond with one of the allowed orderings are assumed to give random responses. Since each of the item-specific error rates for the ordered scale types has specific value (deterministic) constraints imposed on it (equation 4.5), no parameters are estimated for the conditional probabilities of the first $k + 1$ classes, thus no degrees of freedom are used for this part of the analysis. On the other hand, no restrictions are placed on the k item error rates of the unscalable type (the $k + 2$ class); consequently this class requires k degrees of freedom to estimate the conditional probabilities for the k observed measures. An additional $k + 1$ degrees of freedom are required to estimate the proportion of the population in each of the scale types, resulting in a total of $2k + 1$ parameters estimated for this model. The L^2 for this model is reported in Table 4.6. Since the L^2 (20.55, 6 df) is significant, we must reject the Goodman Intrinsically unscalable model. The data do not support the notion that a proportion $1 - \pi_0$ of the population follows a strict Guttman ordering, while π_0 of the population is unscalable.

The Goodman scale model can also be estimated assuming a single response error rate for the $k + 1$ scalable types like that used in the Proctor model. In such a Proctor-Goodman model, the restrictions of equation 4.1 are imposed on the scalable types, and no restrictions are imposed on the unscalable type. This model requires only one degree of freedom more than the number used in the intrinsically unscalable model—to estimate the single response error rate. As we see from the data presented in Table 4.6, this Proctor-Goodman model has too large of an L^2 (20.63, with $5df$) to be accepted and actually nets a slightly poorer fit to the data than the previous Goodman model in which the scale types were deterministically restricted.

The third Goodman scale model example we consider—the biform scale model—relaxes the assumption that the entire population can be characterized by a single ordering of the scale items. For example, we have been assuming that the population can be characterized as being intrinsically scalable with the ordering of (V, I, A, W) for the four campaign activity scale items. Another part of the population, however, may be intrinsically scalable with a different ordering of the four campaign items. To illustrate, let us suppose that there are *two* possible orderings in the population (i.e., two subpopulations with different orderings): pattern A with an ordering of (V, I, A, W) and pattern B with an ordering of (I, V, A, W). Four of the scale types are identical for each of these two pattern orderings: (1,1,1,1), (1,1,1,2), (1,1,2,2), and (2,2,2,2). The Biform model, however, requires that we accept the intrinsically scalable type (2,1,2,2) as well as (1,2,2,2), netting a total of six allowable scale types. The Biform scale model can be viewed as a special case of the latent structure model that can be estimated by leaving the unscalable type unrestricted and imposing the following exact indicator restrictions on the scalable types:

$$
\begin{aligned}
1.0 &= \pi_{11}^{\bar{V}X} = \pi_{11}^{\bar{I}X} = \pi_{11}^{\bar{A}X} = \pi_{11}^{\bar{W}X}, \\
&= \pi_{12}^{\bar{V}X} = \pi_{12}^{\bar{I}X} = \pi_{12}^{\bar{A}X} = \pi_{22}^{\bar{W}X}, \\
&= \pi_{13}^{\bar{V}X} = \pi_{13}^{\bar{I}X} = \pi_{23}^{\bar{A}X} = \pi_{23}^{\bar{W}X}, \\
&= \pi_{14}^{\bar{V}X} = \pi_{24}^{\bar{I}X} = \pi_{24}^{\bar{A}X} = \pi_{24}^{\bar{W}X},
\end{aligned}
\tag{4.6}
$$

$$= \pi_{25}^{\bar{V}X} = \pi_{25}^{\bar{I}X} = \pi_{25}^{\bar{A}X} = \pi_{25}^{\bar{W}X},$$

$$= \pi_{26}^{\bar{V}X} = \pi_{16}^{\bar{I}X} = \pi_{26}^{\bar{A}X} = \pi_{26}^{\bar{W}X}.$$

The L^2 for the Biform scale model, reported in Table 4.6, is 7.02 with 5 degrees of freedom, which indicates that we can accept this model as fitting to the 1980 NES data. Thus the biform model, which has two orderings of the scale items and one intrinsically unscalable class, provides an acceptable characterization for the campaign activities of the 1980 NES postelection respondents.

In estimating the biform model, we find that $\hat{\pi}_2 = 0.00001$, which implies that the second scale type, with the expected response pattern $(1,1,1,2)$, is estimated to have almost no likelihood of occurrence among the scalable portion of the population. (Clogg [1979] notes that the relevant estimate of the proportion of the scalable population is $\hat{\pi}_2/[1 - \hat{\pi}_0]$). This indicates that the Work variable is not useful for distinguishing between scale type 1 $(1,1,1,1)$ and scale type 3 $(1,1,2,2)$. Clogg and Sawyer (1981) show that when a scale type in an acceptable model is estimated to have a very low probability of occurrence, the model can be reestimated excluding that class, with the improvement of fit L^2 being a test of whether the related scale item can be deleted from the set of scale items. For example, since our biform model provides an acceptable fit to the data, the model is reestimated excluding the scale type 2 class, and the results are reported as the final model in Table 4.6. As we see, excluding the scale type 2 class nets an acceptable improvement of fit $(0.25$ with $1df)$. This indicates that the work item can be deleted from the campaign activity scale. The resulting analysis, however, would include only $2^3 = 8$ degrees of freedom, so we conclude the analysis at this point.

As we can see from these four brief examples, the Goodman scale model provides a variety of alternative models for analyzing scales. Those who wish to analyze these types of scale items should consult the Clogg and Sawyer (1981) presentation to gain a full appreciation of the flexibility of the latent class model for scale analysis.

5. COMPARING LATENT STRUCTURES AMONG GROUPS

In previous chapters our discussion focused on the estimation of the latent class model with data collected from a single population or group. This chapter extends our consideration of latent class models to recent developments permitting the comparison of latent structures in multiple groups—what Clogg and Goodman (1984, 1985) refer to as *simultaneous* latent structure analysis in several groups. Simultaneous analysis of latent structures provides a powerful, comparative analytic technique that can be used whenever identical measures are obtained for members of two or more groups. Although we discuss simultaneous analysis for only two groups, the methods presented in this chapter can be readily extended to three or more groups and can also be used for simultaneous scalogram analysis in two or more groups (Clogg and Goodman 1986). Also, simultaneous latent structure analysis can readily be used to study trends in latent structures when the "groups" are independently drawn samples of the same population at different times (McCutcheon 1986).

There are a variety of possible outcomes when the latent structures of two or more groups are compared. At one extreme, the latent structures of the groups may be absolutely heterogeneous—that is, the latent classes in one group may differ in both nature and number from that of the other group(s). We do not consider this type of outcome, other than to note it as a possibility, since it is clear that groups which have a different *number* of latent classes have dissimilar latent structures. The first type of outcome we consider is what Clogg and Goodman refer to as the *heterogeneous, unrestricted T-class model*—when the latent structures in the different groups are found to have the same *number* of classes, with none of the within group parameters (i.e., conditional probabilities and latent class probabilities) being restricted. Under these circumstances, our interest is typically in whether the T latent classes identified in one group are similar in structure to the T classes identified in the other group(s). In terms of the latent class model, we ask whether the same conditional probabilities hold for corresponding classes in each group. If across-group equality restrictions can be imposed on some of the conditional probabilities, we can conclude that the latent structures of the groups are *partially homogeneous* (Clogg and Goodman 1984, 1985), and—depending on the number of restricted parameters—we would be inclined to view the latent structures of the groups as similar to one another. If across-group equality restrictions can be imposed on *all* of the parameters, we can conclude that the latent structures of the groups are *homogeneous*—that the same latent structure occurs in each of the groups. Briefly, an overview of the modeling sequence is: (1) determine the number of classes in each group; (2) if the number of classes are equal, compare the structure (conditional probabilities) of the classes across groups; and (3) if the structure of the classes is the same, check for group differences in the distribution of the population across the latent classes.

The estimation of simultaneous latent structure models in different groups requires modifying the basic latent structure model presented in the previous chapters. In the next section we examine these modifications. In the third section we present a heterogeneous, unrestricted T-class analysis of respondent types, comparing the latent structures of white and black respondents. In the final section we consider homogeneity models in which across-group restrictions are imposed.

SIMULTANEOUS LATENT STRUCTURE MODEL

In the basic latent structure model, several observed variables (e.g., A, B, C) are analyzed to define a latent variable X which has T latent classes. Now consider the case in which the variables A, B, and C have been observed in more than one group. We let G denote the group variable, which is indexed by $s = 1, \ldots, S$. We can think of the combination of observed variables as S separate crosstabulations of $A \times B \times C$—that is, we think of the crosstabulations of the observed variables in the first group $(s = 1)$, the second group $(s = 2)$, and so forth. The model probabilities are calculated on the basis of the total number of observations in all of the groups, so that the proportion of the population in group s can be computed by summing all the probabilities in the crosstabulation of group s:

$$\pi_s^G = \sum_{i,j,k} \pi_{ijks}^{ABCG} \tag{5.1}$$

where

$$\sum_s \pi_s^G = 1.0 \tag{5.2}$$

The conditional probability that an individual in group s is at level (i, j, k) of the crosstabulation is

$$\pi_{ijks}^{\bar{A}\bar{B}\bar{C}G} = \pi_{ijks}^{ABCG} \big/ \pi_s^G \tag{5.3}$$

The conditional probabilities reflect our concern with the probabilities *within* each of S groups. Were there only a single group $(S = 1)$, the conditional probability in equation 5.3 would equal π_{ijk}^{ABC}, since this is the probability that an individual (in the *only* group) is at level (i, j, k). When $S \geq 2$, however, the focus must be on probabilities that are specific to each of the S groups so that between-group comparisons can be made. Thus, when $S \geq 2$, and there is a T-class latent structure in each of the S groups, equation 2.10 can be rewritten as

$$\pi_{ijks}^{\bar{A}\bar{B}\bar{C}G} = \sum_t \pi_{ijkst}^{\bar{A}\bar{B}\bar{C}G\bar{X}} \tag{5.4}$$

This states that for an individual in group s, the probability of being at level (i, j, k) is equal to the sum over the T latent classes of the conditional probabilities of being at level (i, j, k, t) of the observed and latent variables.

$$\pi_{ijkst}^{\bar{A}\bar{B}\bar{C}G\bar{X}} = \pi_{ist}^{\bar{A}GX} \times \pi_{jst}^{\bar{B}GX} \times \pi_{kst}^{\bar{C}GX} \times \pi_{st}^{G\bar{X}} \tag{5.5}$$

This is a modification of equation 2.7 which says that, for individuals in group s, the probability of being at level (i, j, k, t) on the latent and observed variables is equal to the product of (1) the conditional probabilities for each of the observed measures for latent class t in group s, and (2) the conditional latent class probability of being in latent class t for members of group s. Each of these probabilities is specific to the level (s) of the group variable (G).

Within each group, the conditional latent class probabilities (i.e., the probability of an individual being in a particular class) sum to 1.0

$$\sum_t \pi_{st}^{G\bar{X}} = 1.0 \qquad (5.6)$$

and, within each of the latent classes for each of the groups, the conditional probabilities for each observed measure sum to 1.0

$$\sum_i \pi_{ist}^{\bar{A}GX} = \sum_j \pi_{jst}^{\bar{B}GX} = \sum_k \pi_{kst}^{\bar{C}GX} \qquad (5.7)$$

The restrictions of 5.6 indicate that $T - 1$ latent classes must be estimated for each of the S groups, and that $(I-1)+(J-1)+(K-1)$ conditional probabilities must be estimated for each of the T classes and S groups. Thus the number of estimated parameters for the unrestricted heterogeneous T-class model is

$$\begin{aligned} S(T-1) + [ST(I-1) + ST(J-1) + ST(K-1)] \\ = S[(I+J+K-2)T-1] \end{aligned} \qquad (5.8)$$

There are some important differences between simultaneous latent structure analysis and the latent structure analysis model presented in the previous chapters. In latent structure analysis, we attempt to estimate the probability that an individual is in latent class t, noting that we must estimate $T-1$ latent class probabilities. In simultaneous latent structure analysis, we attempt to estimate the probability that an individual *in group s* is in latent class t. As equations 5.4–5.6 indicate, we must now estimate $S(T-1)$ latent class probabilities, since within different groups, respondents may be distributed differently among the T latent classes. For example, in our earlier analysis of respondent types, we attempted to estimate the proportion of white respondents whom we would classify as skeptics. In a simultaneous latent structure analysis of white and black respondent types, however, we must attempt to estimate the proportion of white respondents *and* the proportion of black respondents whom we would classify as skeptics, since the members of these two groups (populations) may be differentially likely to be skeptical of surveys.

A second, and in some ways more significant, difference between simultaneous latent structure analysis and the latent structure analysis presented earlier has to do with the estimation of the conditional probabilities. In latent structure analysis, we estimate the probability that individuals in latent class t will be at level i of measure A $(\pi_{it}^{\bar{A}X})$, level j of measure B $(\pi_{jt}^{\bar{B}X})$, and so forth. We must estimate a separate conditional probability for all but the final level of each measure, for each of the latent classes—for example, we must estimate $(I-1)T$ separate conditional probabilities for variable A. These conditional probabilities are then used to help us characterize each of the classes of the latent variable. In simultaneous latent structure analysis, we estimate the probability that individuals *in group* s, who are also in latent class t, will be at level i of measure A $(\pi_{ist}^{\bar{A}GX})$, level j of measure B $(\pi_{jst}^{\bar{B}GX})$, and so forth. For variable A we must now estimate $(I-1)ST$ separate conditional probabilities, because the probability of being at level i on measure A may be different for individuals in latent class t of one group than it is for individuals in latent class t in another group. Moreover, differences between the groups' conditional probabilities may indicate the existence of fundamentally different latent structures in the groups. For example, if we found that white respondents in the third latent class were highly likely to respond that surveys are a waste of time and money, and that black respondents in the third latent class were highly *unlikely* to respond that surveys are a waste, we would be reluctant to conclude that the third latent class is identical for white and black respondents.

The simultaneous latent structure model requires the estimation of $S \times T$ latent classes and $S \times T$ conditional probabilities for each level of the observed measures, even though the model that we have presented thus far indexes only T latent classes. For example, while we discuss three latent classes of respondent types, we must estimate *six* latent classes: three for the white respondents and three for the black respondents. In general terms, when a T-class simultaneous latent structure is estimated for S groups, the first set of T latent classes $(1, 2, \ldots, T)$ refers to the first group $(s = 1)$, the next set of T latent classes $(T+1, T+2, \ldots, 2T)$ refers to the second group $(s = 2)$, and so forth to the final set of T latent classes $([S-1]T+1, [S-1]T+2, \ldots, ST)$, which refers to the Sth group. Thus the latent variable X is *doubly* subscripted in simultaneous latent structure models: one subscript for the class (t) and another for the group (s).

Clogg and Goodman (1984, 1985) suggest an alternative formulation of the simultaneous latent structure model which simplifies the notation. They propose defining a variable $Y = G \times X$, which is the crosstabulation of the group variable and the latent variable. Variable Y has U levels, where $U = ST$. Since the latent variable X is nested within Y, variable Y is also a latent variable. There is a correspondence between the levels u of Y and the levels (s, t) of $G \times X$:

$$u = [1, 2, \ldots, T, T + 1, \ldots, U]$$
$$(s, t) = [(1, 1), (1, 2), \ldots, (1, T), (2, 1), \ldots, (S, T)] \tag{5.9}$$

This correspondence means that

$$Y_1 = G_1 X_1; Y_2 = G_1 X_2; \ldots; Y_T = G_1 X_T; Y_{T+1} = G_2 X_1;$$
$$Y_{T+2} = G_2 X_2; \ldots; Y_U = G_S X_T$$

The value of u can be readily determined as $u = (s - 1)T + t$.

The advantage of defining the latent variable Y in this manner is that the simultaneous latent structure model can now be expressed in terms similar to those for the usual latent class model:

$$\pi_{ijks}^{ABCG} = \sum_u \pi_{ijksu}^{ABCGY} \tag{5.10}$$

This says that the joint probabilities of the $A \times B \times C \times G$ crosstabulation are distributed over the U latent classes, similar to equation 2.10. And, like equation 2.7, the probability π_{ijksu}^{ABCGY} equals the product of latent class and conditional probabilities:

$$\pi_{ijksu}^{ABCGY} = \pi_u^Y \times \pi_{iu}^{\bar{A}Y} \times \pi_{ju}^{\bar{B}Y} \times \pi_{ku}^{\bar{C}Y} \times \pi_{su}^{\bar{G}Y} \tag{5.11}$$

By imposing deterministic restrictions on the $\pi_{su}^{\bar{G}Y}$, this model enables the estimation of simultaneous latent structures. The restrictions are of the nature:

$$\pi_{su}^{\bar{G}Y} = 1.0, \quad for \quad u = (s - 1)T + t \quad (t = 1, \ldots, T)$$
$$\pi_{su}^{\bar{G}Y} = 0.0, \quad for \quad u \neq (s - 1)T + t \quad (t = 1, \ldots, T) \tag{5.12}$$

That is, we impose restrictions on the model conditional probabilities such that individuals in the first set of T latent classes $(u = 1, \ldots, T)$ have a 1.0 probability of being in the first group $(s = 1)$ and a 0 probability of being in any other group; individuals in the second set of T latent classes $(u = T + 1, \ldots, 2T)$ have a 1.0 probability of being in the second group $(s = 2)$ and a 0 probability of being in any other group; and so forth to the last set of T latent classes $(u = [S - 1]T + 1, \ldots, U)$ which have a 1.0 probability of being in the Sth group and a 0 probability of being in any other group. These restrictions make it possible to simultaneously estimate the latent structures in several groups by enabling the estimation of $U = ST$ latent classes, and they reflect the fact that T is nested in G in the latent variable Y.

Clogg and Goodman (1984, 1985) also note that:

$$\pi_{iu}^{\bar{A}Y} = \pi_{ist}^{\bar{A}GX} \tag{5.13}$$

$$\pi_{ju}^{\bar{B}Y} = \pi_{jst}^{\bar{B}GX} \tag{5.15}$$

$$\pi_{ku}^{\bar{C}Y} = \pi_{kst}^{\bar{C}GX} \tag{5.16}$$

$$\pi_{u}^{Y} = \pi_{st}^{G\bar{X}}\pi_{s}^{G} \tag{5.17}$$

These indicate that the conditional probabilities for the observed measures (A, B, C) under the deterministically restricted model are identical to those presented earlier. Rearranging equation 5.17 allows us to define the conditional latent class probabilities for each of the S groups:

$$\pi_{st}^{G\bar{X}} = \pi_{u}^{Y} \Big/ \pi_{s}^{G} \tag{5.18}$$

where

$$\sum_{u=(s-1)T+1}^{sT} \pi_{u}^{Y} = \pi_{s}^{G} \tag{5.19}$$

Later, we will see that when the conditional probabilities for the observed measures in each latent class are either identical or very similar for the several groups, the conditional latent class probabilities can be used to compare groups on the basis of the proportion of the members found to occur in each of the latent types.

HETEROGENEOUS T-CLASS MODEL

In this section we return to the analysis of respondent types, this time focusing on a simultaneous latent structure analysis of black and white respondents (i.e., $S = 2$). The data for the example are from the 1982 General Social Survey oversample of blacks, which is a national probability sample of 510 black Americans (Davis and Smith 1985). Specific question wordings and the crosstabulation of the data for the white respondents are reported in Chapter 3 (Table 3.1). The crosstabulation for the black respondents is presented in Table 5.1; as with the white respondents, black respondents are excluded if any of the four measures are missing. This results in an effective sample size of 447 blacks from the 1982 GSS.

We begin by estimating the unrestricted, heterogeneous three-class model—meaning that we estimate three latent classes for the white respondents and three latent classes for the black respondents, for a total of six latent classes ($U = S \times T = 2 \times 3$). Following the practice from Chapter 3 of referring to the four observed measures as P, A, U, C, which are indexed by i, j, k, l respectively, we see that $S[(I + J + K + L - 3)T - 1] = 2[(3 + 2 + 2 + 3 - 3)3 - 1] = 40$ nonredundant parameters must be estimated for this model. The estimated parameters for the unrestricted, heterogeneous three-class model of black and white respondent types are reported in Table 5.2.

The L^2 for this model of black and white respondent types ($39.690, 31df$) indicates that the unrestricted, heterogeneous three-class model provides an adequate fit to the observed data. We should note that when parameters are estimated as .000, it is the usual practice to reclaim "their" degrees of freedom for the test—thus we could claim 34 degrees of freedom for the model L^2 test.

A comparison of the Table 5.2 parameters for white respondents with the parameters presented in Table 3.3 indicates that the conditional probabilities and (conditional) latent class probabilities are nearly identical. This is because the estimation of unrestricted, homogeneous T-class models is equivalent to estimating separate

Table 5.1: Cross-tabulation of Observed Variables for Black Respondents: 1982 GSS

PURPOSE	ACCURACY	UNDERSTANDING	COOPERATION		
			Interested	Cooperative	Impatient, Hostile
Good	Mostly True	Good	117	14	3
		Fair, Poor	34	19	5
	Not True	Good	95	10	3
		Fair, Poor	23	14	2
Depends	Mostly True	Good	7	1	0
		Fair, Poor	3	1	0
	Not True	Good	19	1	2
		Fair, Poor	2	1	1
Waste	Mostly True	Good	6	0	0
		Fair, Poor	3	1	0
	Not True	Good	30	9	1
		Fair, Poor	9	7	4

Table 5.2: Estimated Parameters for the Unrestricted, Heterogeneous Three-Class Model: White and Black Respondent Types: 1982 GSS

Manifest Variables		Whites			Blacks	
		(I)	(II)	(III)	(I)	(II)	(III)
P	Good	.888	.912	.143	.865	.905	.100
	Depends	.053	.072	.225	.085	.047	.178
	Waste	.059	.017	.633	.050	.048	.722
A	Mostly True	.613	.648	.031	.524	.622	.000*
	Not True	.387	.352	.969	.476	.378	1.000
C	Interested	.943	.690	.641	.991	.590	.634
	Cooperative	.057	.255	.256	.004	.341	.252
	Impatient,						
	Hostile	.000*	.055	.103	.005	.069	.114
U	Good	1.000	.313	.753	.993	.397	.678
	Fair, Poor	.000*	.687	.247	.007	.603	.322
Latent Class Probabilities		.4525	.1508	.1256	.1226	.1052	.0432
Conditional Latent Class Probabilities		.6208	.2069	.1723	.4524	.3882	.1594

(Header: Respondent Type)

* Estimated as .000 by maximum likelihood procedure.

unrestricted latent structure models for each of the s groups, and underscores the equivalence of equations 2.7 and 5.5—the first estimates the latent structure in one group, and the second estimates the simultaneous latent structures in several groups. For white respondents, only the latent class probabilities differ between Tables 3.3 and 5.2 due to the fact that the latent class probabilities in simultaneous latent structure analysis are calculated over all of the groups (equation 5.2).

In the lower section of Table 5.2 are reported both latent class probabilities and *conditional* latent class probabilities. When groups are of unequal size $(\pi_1^G \neq \pi_2^G \neq \ldots \neq \pi_S^G)$, the conditional latent class probabilities (π_{st}^{GX}) are more useful than the latent class probabilities (π_u^Y) for group comparisons on the relative distributions of individuals in each of the T classes. As equation 5.18 indicates, the conditional latent class probabilities can be calculated by dividing each latent class probability by the proportion of the population in the corresponding group (π_s^G). We can calculate the probability of being in each of the groups $(\pi_1^G$ and $\pi_2^G)$ by summing the latent class probabilities from $(s-1)T + 1$ to sT. For whites $(s = 1)$ we sum latent class probabilities $([s-1]T+1 = [1-1]3+1 =)$ 1 to $(sT = 1 \times 3 =)$ 3, and for blacks $(s = 2)$ we sum latent class probabilities $([s - 1]T + 1 = [2 - 1]3 + 1 =)$ 4 to $(sT = 2 \times 3 =)$ 6. Thus the proportion of the population that is white (π_1^G) is $(.4525 + .1508 + .1256 =) .7289$, and the proportion of the population that is black (π_2^G) is $(.1226 + .1052 + .0432 =) .2710$—within the limits of rounding error, these proportions sum to 1.0. Each of the conditional latent class probabilities for the white respondent classes, then, is calculated by dividing the latent class probabilities by .7289, and the conditional latent class probabilities for black respondents are calculated by dividing the latent class probabilities by .2710.

The conditional latent class probabilities in Table 5.2 indicate that whites are more likely than blacks to be in latent classes I and III, and that blacks are more likely than whites to be in class II. A quick inspection of the conditional probabilities for each of the classes of the two groups, however, indicates that an interpretation of these conditional latent class probabilities will be highly ambiguous. Although the conditional probabilities for each of the classes of the two groups appear to be similar, with the heterogeneous T-class model we cannot be certain that the classes of one group are *the same as* those of another group. Consequently, we may wish to impose across-group equality constraints on the conditional probabilities to test whether the classes of one group have the same relations to the observed measures as the classes of another group. Clogg and Goodman (1984, 1985) refer to simultaneous latent structure models with across-group equality constraints as *homogeneity* models.

HOMOGENEITY MODELS

Clogg and Goodman (1984, 1985) distinguish between *partial* and *complete* homogeneity models in simultaneous latent structure analysis. Latent structures are partially homogeneous when across-group equality constraints are imposed on *some* of the conditional probabilities and conditional latent class probabilities. They are completely homogeneous when the latent classes of all of the groups are identical—when across-group equality constraints can be imposed on *all* of the conditional probabilities and conditional latent class probabilities.

Across-group equality constraints on the conditional probabilities are usually the first type of restrictions to be examined in the sequence of tests. These constraints allow us to test hypotheses regarding the similarity of the groups' latent structures by testing whether the probability of responding affirmatively (or negatively) to each question is similar for corresponding classes in all groups. Consequently, across-group equality constraints on the conditional latent class probabilities are considered last, since we usually wish to know if the groups' classes are similar in structure before we test whether the proportion of the population in each class is similar across groups. Across-group equality constraints on the conditional probabilities are usually of the type

$$\pi_{i1t}^{\bar{A}GX} = \pi_{i2t}^{\bar{A}GX} = \ldots = \pi_{iSt}^{\bar{A}GX} \qquad (5.20)$$

for any of the observed variables. Note that it is not necessary to impose an equality constraint on all of the groups simultaneously: equality constraints may be imposed for as few as two groups.

Completely homogeneous latent structures may be estimated incrementally, beginning with the heterogeneous T-class model and testing partially homogeneous models by restricting a few additional parameters at a time. The L^2 of the model that lacks the newly imposed restrictions can be subtracted from the L^2 of the partial homogeneity model with the additional restrictions to obtain an improvement of fit L^2, with degrees of freedom being equal to the difference in the corresponding models' degrees of freedom. It is important to note that when several additional restrictions are imposed at once, a multiple degree of freedom improvement of fit L^2 may appear to provide an acceptable fit while actually masking unacceptable restrictions. Consequently, when an improvement of fit L^2 with several degrees of freedom is found to be acceptable, but the L^2 value exceeds the a priori criterion for statistical significance (e.g., $p < .05$) for one degree of freedom, the model should be reestimated with fewer restrictions to ensure that all of the restrictions are individually acceptable. The results of this type of incremental fitting procedure for the simultaneous latent structure analysis of black and white respondent types are presented in Table 5.3.

Table 5.3: L^2 and Decisions for Simultaneous Latent Class
Models of White and Black Respondent Types: 198 GSS

Model	L^2	χ^2	Degrees of Freedom
Unrestricted, Heterogeneous T-class Model	39.69	39.24	33
Partial Homogeneity Models			
H_1	39.95	40.19	36
H_2	40.18	40.45	41
H_3	42.84	43.33	45
H_4	44.00	44.05	47
H_5	45.93	45.96	48
H_6	47.42	46.66	49
H_7	47.43	46.57	50
H_8	49.82	49.01	51
H_9	51.73	50.62	54
H_{10}	53.10	53.23	56
Restricted, Complete Homogeneity Model	97.99	99.77	58

As the information in Table 5.3 indicates, we have reclaimed
the three degrees of freedom for the three parameters estimated to
be .00 in the unrestricted, heterogeneous three-class model (Table
5.2). The first set of across-group equality constraints we impose
(H_1) is on the three parameters estimated to be zero in the heterogeneity model

$$\pi_{113}^{\bar{A}GX} = \pi_{123}^{\bar{A}GX} = \pi_{311}^{\bar{C}GX} = \pi_{321}^{\bar{C}GX} = \pi_{211}^{\bar{U}GX} = \pi_{221}^{\bar{U}GX} = 0.$$

The improvement of fit L^2 ($39.95 - 39.69 = 0.26, 3df$) indicates
that these constraints provide an acceptable fit. Next (H_2), five
across-group equality constraints are imposed

$$\pi_{111}^{\bar{P}GX} = \pi_{121}^{\bar{P}GX}, \pi_{112}^{\bar{P}GX} = \pi_{122}^{\bar{P}GX}, \pi_{113}^{\bar{P}GX} = \pi_{123}^{\bar{P}GX},$$
$$\pi_{113}^{\bar{C}GX} = \pi_{123}^{\bar{C}GX}, \pi_{213}^{\bar{C}GX} = \pi_{223}^{\bar{C}GX}$$

These conditional probabilities are selected for equality constraints
because their estimates under H_1 were very similar in each group.
The improvement of fit $L^2(H_2|H_1) = 0.23$ with 5 degrees of free-

dom indicates that the five additional constraints are acceptable. This process is repeated as additional across-group equality constraints are imposed on the simultaneous latent structures. We examine the estimates of the conditional probabilities under the current model and impose across-group equality restrictions on those which appear to be of similar magnitude in each group. In H_3 we impose four across-group constraints in addition to those we imposed on the model in H_2:

$$\pi_{112}^{\bar{A}GX} = \pi_{122}^{\bar{A}GX}, \pi_{211}^{\bar{P}GX} = \pi_{221}^{\bar{P}GX}, \pi_{212}^{\bar{P}GX} = \pi_{222}^{\bar{P}GX},$$
$$\pi_{312}^{\bar{C}GX} = \pi_{322}^{\bar{C}GX}$$

As before, the addition of these across-group equality restrictions results in an acceptable improvement of fit—$L^2(H_3|H_2) = 2.66$ with four degrees of freedom.

Each of the additional across-group equality restrictions indicates acceptable improvements of fit for H_4–H_8. The test of H_8 indicates that all of the conditional probabilities in each of the three latent classes are identical across the two groups—that is, the first latent class in the white group is identical in structure to the first class in the black group, the second class in the white group is identical to the second class in the black group, and the third class is also identical in the two groups. The set of restrictions imposed in H_9 tests the hypothesis that the subjective evaluations of surveys—Accuracy and Purpose—among class I (ideal) respondents is identical to the subjective evaluations of class II respondents (believers). The prior across-group equality constraints means that these across-class constraints also translate into across-group constraints:

$$\pi_{111}^{\bar{A}GX} = \pi_{112}^{\bar{A}GX} = \pi_{121}^{\bar{A}GX} = \pi_{122}^{\bar{A}GX}$$
$$\pi_{111}^{\bar{P}GX} = \pi_{112}^{\bar{P}GX} = \pi_{121}^{\bar{P}GX} = \pi_{122}^{\bar{P}GX}$$
$$\pi_{211}^{\bar{P}GX} = \pi_{212}^{\bar{P}GX} = \pi_{221}^{\bar{P}GX} = \pi_{222}^{\bar{P}GX}$$

Clogg and Goodman (1984, 1985) refer to models with across-class equality constraints as *restricted*, which means that H_9 represents a restricted, partially homogeneous model. The $L^2(H_9|H_8) = 1.91$ with three degrees of freedom, indicating an acceptable fit.

In H_{10} we impose across-group equality constraints on the conditional latent class probabilities of class III. This restriction tests whether there is a significant difference in the relative frequency of class III type respondents among the white and black groups.

$$\pi_{13}^{G\bar{X}} = \pi_{23}^{G\bar{X}}$$

The improvement of fit $L^2(H_{10}|H_9) = 1.37$ with two degrees of freedom indicates that there is no significant difference between the probabilities that whites and blacks are class III type respondents.

Finally, we test whether there are any significant differences between the white and black groups with regard to respondent types—the completely homogeneous model. Given that we have already imposed across-group restrictions on all of the parameters other than the class I and class II conditional latent class probabilities (H_{10}), and that only one of these parameters is nonredundant (equation 5.6), this one degree of freedom test provides an efficient test of the hypothesis that whites and blacks are differentially distributed in classes I and II. The large increase in the L^2 (44.89, $2df$) indicates that restricting whites and blacks to being equally distributed in classes I and II causes the model to differ significantly from the data. Therefore, we must reject the complete homogeneity simultaneous latent structure model. The characteristics of each of these classes can be seen from the data in Table 5.4.

Since the conditional probabilities for race $(\pi_{su}^{\bar{G}Y})$ are deterministically restricted to 1.0 and 0.0—where the probability of being in the white group is 1.0 for whites and 0.0 for blacks, while the probability of being in the black group is 0.0 for whites and 1.0 for blacks—these conditional probabilities are not reported. Similar to the findings reported in Chapter 3, the remaining conditional probabilities indicate that the three classes can be characterized as ideal respondents (class I), believers (class II), and skeptics (class III).

Among the ideal respondents and believers, 9 of 10 (.890) are likely to respond that surveys serve a good Purpose, while fewer than 1 of 6 (.172) of the skeptics report similar evaluations of surveys. Indeed, more than 3 of 5 (.615) skeptics report believing that

Table 5.4: Estimated Parameters for the Restricted, Partially Homogeneous Model: White and Black Respondent Types: 1982 GSS

Manifest Variables		Whites			Blacks	
	(I)	(II)	(III)	(I)	(II)	(III)
P Good	.890†	.890†	.172	.890†	.890†	.172
Depends	.059†	.059†	.213	.059†	.059†	.213
Waste	.051	.051	.615	.051	.051	.615
A Mostly True	.618†	.618†	.000*	.618†	.618†	.000*
Not True	.382	.382	1.000	.382	.382	1.000
C Interested	.949	.648	.662	.949	.648	.662
Cooperative	.051	.288	.237	.051	.288	.237
Impatient, Hostile	.000*	.064	.100	.000*	.064	.100
U Good	1.000	.331	.752	1.000	.331	.752
Fair, Poor	.000*	.669	.248	.000*	.669	.248
Latent Class Probabilities	.4424	.1550	.1315‡	.1250	.0972	.0489‡
Conditional Latent Class Probabilities	.6069	.2127	.1804‡	.4610	.3585	.1804‡

*Restricted to .000.
†Across-class equality restriction.
‡Across-group equality restriction on latent class probability.

surveys are a waste of time and money. Additionally, while skeptics are uniformly likely to report that surveys are Accurate only some of the time or hardly ever, more than 3 of 5 (.618) ideal respondents and believers are likely to report that surveys are Accurate always or most of the time. As we found in Chapter 3, ideal respondents are likely to have been evaluated by the interviewers as friendly and interested (.949) with good understanding (1.000). Believers and skeptics are less likely to have been evaluated as friendly and interested (.648 and .662, respectively), and 1 of 10 (.100) skeptics was evaluated by interviewers as being impatient and restless or hostile. Finally, 3 of 4 (.752) skeptics are likely to have been evaluated as having good Understanding of the survey questions, while only 1 of 3 (.331) of the believers is likely to have been rated this way.

The equivalence of the latent structures for whites and blacks is indicated by our ability to impose across-group equality restrictions on the conditional probabilities of all of the observed measures. That is, we can classify white and black respondents with the same three characterizations: ideal respondents, believers, and skeptics. Moreover, the acceptability of an across-group equality constraint on the latent class probability of class III suggests that an equal proportion of whites and blacks are likely to be skeptical of surveys. Latent class probability restrictions, such as the across group equality constraint on skeptics, are actually imposed on the *conditional* latent class probabilities $(\pi_{st}^{G\bar{X}})$. Consequently, when the groups are of unequal size (i.e., $\pi_1^G \neq \pi_2^G \neq \ldots \neq \pi_S^G$), the equality of latent class probabilities is most evident among the conditional latent class probabilities, as we see between the conditional latent class probabilities of skeptics for whites and blacks (both equal .1804).

The unacceptability of an across-group equality constraint on the latent class probabilities of the ideal respondents and the believers indicates a significant difference in the distribution of whites and blacks in these categories. Specifically, it appears that blacks are more likely than whites to be classified as believers (.3585 and .2127, respectively), and whites are more likely than blacks to be classified as ideal respondents (.6069 and .4610, respectively). This finding raises important methodological questions regarding the validity of survey results in different populations. The differences may simply reflect racial differences in educational attainment, since the better educated should be more likely to understand the questions. Importantly, however, these results may indicate that surveys are less valid for blacks than whites, either because the instruments are culturally biased (and less likely to be understood by blacks) or because survey interviewers evaluate black and white respondents differently.

SPECIAL APPLICATIONS OF SIMULTANEOUS LATENT STRUCTURE ANALYSIS

Although a complete presentation of the variety of the uses of simultaneous latent structure analysis is beyond the scope of this paper, we briefly mention two additional applications recently suggested by Clogg and Goodman. We can compare the scalability of a set of items in two or more populations (Clogg and Goodman 1986) by imposing across-class restrictions (Chapter 4) within the groups of the heterogeneous T-class model $(T = k + 1)$ and imposing across-group equality constraints on the conditional probabilities (error rates). Also, across-group equality constraints can be imposed on the latent class probabilities to compare the distribution of the groups over the scale scores. Clogg and Goodman (1984) suggest that simultaneous latent structure analysis can also be used to analyze quasi-independence models, such as those presented in "turnover" tables. An example of such a table is one that represents individuals' responses to the same question at two different times—variable A (indexed by $i = 1, \ldots, I$) is the response given at time 1, and variable B (indexed by $j = 1, \ldots, J$) is the response given at time 2. The cross-classification of variables $A \times B$ nets a square table $(I = J)$ in which individuals giving consistent responses are all located on the main diagonal $(i = j)$.

When $A \times B$ tables are available in two or more populations, Clogg and Goodman suggest estimating $I + 1$ latent classes (i.e., $T = I + 1$) in which the first $T - 1$ classes for each group are restricted to include only those individuals with consistent answers $(i = j)$

$$\pi_{1s1}^{\bar{A}GX} = \pi_{1s1}^{\bar{B}GX} = 1.0$$
$$\pi_{2s2}^{\bar{A}GX} = \pi_{2s2}^{\bar{B}GX} = 1.0$$
$$\vdots \qquad \vdots \qquad\qquad (5.21)$$
$$\pi_{(T-1)s(T-1)}^{\bar{A}GX} = \pi_{(T-1)s(T-1)}^{\bar{B}GX} = 1.0$$

No restrictions are imposed on latent class T. As a consequence of the restrictions on the first $T - 1$ latent classes, the conditional latent class probabilities of these latent classes $(\pi_{s1}^{G\bar{X}}, \ldots, \pi_{s(T-1)}^{G\bar{X}})$ represent the proportion of intrinsically consistent respondents for each response level $(1, \ldots, i)$, and the conditional latent class probability of class T $(\pi_{sT}^{G\bar{X}})$ represents the intrinsically inconsistent responses for the groups. Many other tests for turnover tables can also be made using the types of across-group restrictions discussed in this chapter.

6. CONCLUSIONS

Although latent class analysis has been described as a qualitative data analog to factor analysis (Green 1951, 1952), recent developments using the latent class model have proven the model to be far more flexible than this early assessment indicates. As we have seen, the latent class model can indeed function as a qualitative data analogue to factor analysis, in *exploratory* (unrestricted) and a *confirmatory* (restricted) analyses in a single group, as well as in comparative (*simultaneous*) analyses of the latent structures of several groups. The latent class model, however, does not require the assumption from factor analysis that the data have multivariate normal distributions. Since the social world seems to have been created with less multivariate normality than many researchers are willing to assume, it is likely that latent class analysis will continue to enjoy an increasingly prominent role in social research.

We have also seen that the latent class model is a highly flexible analytic method for scalogram analysis. The latent class model can be used to test a wide variety of hypotheses concerning response error and the scalability of items. By combining the response error restrictions of scalogram analysis with across-group restrictions, researchers may conduct simultaneous scalogram analysis of items in several groups (Clogg and Goodman 1986).

The flexibility of the latent class model has also been used in ways which we have not explored. One of these usages which seems to offer substantial promise for further development is the use of latent class models to analyze quasi-independence models such as are found in "turnover" tables. Clogg (1981b) and Marsden (1985) have shown the latent class model to be a powerful method for the analysis of intergenerational occupational mobility turnover tables. This approach should prove especially useful for the analysis of panel data and intergenerational analysis (e.g., political and religious socialization). Additionally, Clogg and Goodman (1984) indicate that the simultaneous latent class model can be used to make across-group comparisons of such quasi-independence models.

One other usage of the latent class model is in the analysis of causal relations among latent variables. While this method has yet to be fully exploited by researchers, Clogg (1981a), Madden and Dillon (1982), and Bergen (1983) demonstrate that the latent class model can be used to estimate path coefficients between latent variables to explain relationships observed between the measured variables. In general, the latent class model provides a powerful and flexible method for analyzing the causal structure of relations among qualitative measures without requiring assumptions about the normality of the variables' distributions.

NOTES

[1] The reader should note that this is the usual method for estimating the Pearson "Goodness-of-fit" chi-square statistic. Although the symbol 'χ^2' actually denotes a distribution, not the estimate of a statistic, we will follow the convention of using this symbol to indicate the estimate of the Goodness-of-fit chi-square statistic.

[2] The GSS is an annual cross-sectional, representative survey of English-speaking persons 18 years of age or over, who live in noninstitutional arrangements within the continental United States (Davis and Smith 1985).

[3] The NES is a biennial cross-sectional pre- and postelection survey of English-speaking persons 18 years of age or over, who live in noninstitutional settings within the continental United States (Miller 1982).

APPENDIX A

This appendix documents the control cards that are required to run the MLLSA program and are reprinted from Clogg's program manual (1977). Examples of the use of many of these control cards can be found in the programs included in Appendix B. The MLLSA program has been adapted by Scott Eliason (MLLSAPC) for use with DOS 2.1 (or higher) on microcomputers having 384K or more of active memory. Copies of the Fortran source code for the MLLSA mainframe and executable MLLSAPC microcomputer programs may be purchased from:

Clifford C. Clogg
Department of Sociology
The Pennsylvania State University
University Park, Pennsylvania 16802

CARD TYPE	COLUMNS [FORMAT]	DESCRIPTION
1. Title (required)	1–80 [20A4]	Enter anything in columns 1–80 to identify the run.
2. Problem Card (required)	1–2 [I2]	Number of manifest variables.
	3–4 [I2]	Number of latent classes.
	5–10 [F6.0]	Sample size—an option allowing a check on the correctness of the input data (optional).

11–16 [I6]	Maximum number of iterations allowed, default is 500 (optional).
17–24 [F8.7]	Maximum deviation to end iterations, default is 5.0×10^{-5} (optional).
25–26 [I2]	Enter 1 if L^2 and χ^2 of independence model is desired (optional).
27–28 [I2]	Enter 1 if automatic assignment of respondents into latent classes is desired (optional).
29–30 [I2]	Enter 1 if parameter estimates are to be punched out (useful in trial stages) (optional).
31–32 [I2]	Enter 1 if variable labels will be entered (See Card Type 4 below) (optional).
33–34 [I2]	Enter 1 if variable value labels will be entered (see card Type 5 below) (optional).
35–36 [I2]	Enter 1 if the model is to have restrictions on the latent class probabilities (π_t^X). See Card Type 10 below (optional).
37–38 [I2]	Enter 1 if the model is to have restrictions on the conditional probabilities (e.g., $\pi_{it}^{\bar{A}X}$). See Card Type 11 below (optional).

	39–40 [I2]	Enter 1 if iteration detail is desired (from the first and last iterations) (optional).
	41–42 [I2]	Enter 1 if output of standard ized residuals is desired (optional).
	43–44 [I2]	Enter 1 if start values are to be the final estimates of the previous problem. Must be blank for first problem in a run. If '1' is entered in 43–44, then 31–34 *must* be *blank*, and sample size must be entered in columns 5–10 (optional).
	45–46 [I2]	Enter 1 if output of column rank and degrees of freedom are desired. If '1' is entered in 39–40, the matrix of derivatives is also output (optional).
	47–48 [I2]	Enter number of groups if simultaneous latent model is to be estimated. The group variable must be entered as the last manifest variable—data must be entered in a group—by—group manner (optional).
3. Classes per variable (required)	1–80 [40I2]	Enter the number of classes of the first variable in columns 1–2, the number of

84

classes in the second variable in columns 3–4, etc.

4. Variable
Labels
(optional*)

1–80
[10(4x,A4)]

*Must use if columns 31–32
of Type 2 card is not blank.
Enter the alphabetic or numeric
variable names: name of first
variable in columns 5–8, name
of second variable in columns
13–16, etc.

5. Value Labels
(optional*)

1–80
[10(4x,A4)]

*Must use if columns 33–34
of Type 2 card is not blank.
If variable labels are used,
value labels may or may not
be used. However, value labels
may *not* be used if
variable labels are not used.
One card for each variable:
enter the label for category 1
in columns 4–8; the label for
category 2 in columns 13–16; etc.
Value labels for *each* variable
must be supplied if this option is
used.

6. Data Format
Card
(required)

1–80
[20A4]

Format of data, e.g., '(8F5.0)'

7. Input Data
(required)

The format
must be

Data must be entered in
'Fortran' order, with the

	identical to that entered in the Type 6 card above.	subscripts associated with the first variable varying most rapidly, those of the second variable varying next most rapidly, etc. *Example*: for the 4–way table with all variables dichotomous, where (i,j,k,l) refers to $(ABCD)$, and A is the first variable, enter the crosstab frequencies frequencies in the order $(1,1,1,1)$, $(2,1,1,1),(1,2,1,1),(2,2,1,1)$, $(1,1,2,1),\ldots,(2,2,2,2)$.
8. Input start values for the latent class probabilities (π_t^X) (required)	1–80 [10F8.7]	Enter initial values for $\hat{\pi}_1^X$ in columns 1–8 (left justified); for $\hat{\pi}_2^X$ in columns 9–16; etc. Enter all T start values where 'T'is the number of latent classes. If necessary, continue entering start values on additional cards until all T values are entered.
9. Input start values for the conditional probabilities (required)	1–80 [10F8.7]	Enter initial values for the conditional probabilities. On the first card, enter $\hat{\pi}_{it}^{\bar{A}X}$, with the classes of A varying most rapidly. Use as many cards as necessary, given the format, to include *all* $I \times T$ start values for $\pi_{it}^{\bar{A}X}$. Then begin a new card for the second variable, etc. Include start values for all conditional probabilities.

Example: For a three-class model with four dichotomous variables, enter the following start values, using the format (10F8.7):

1st card: $\hat{\pi}_{11}^{\bar{A}X}$ $\hat{\pi}_{21}^{\bar{A}X}$ $\hat{\pi}_{12}^{\bar{A}X}$ $\hat{\pi}_{22}^{\bar{A}X}$ $\hat{\pi}_{13}^{\bar{A}X}$ $\hat{\pi}_{13}^{\bar{A}X}$

2nd card: $\hat{\pi}_{11}^{\bar{B}X}$ $\hat{\pi}_{21}^{\bar{B}X}$ $\hat{\pi}_{12}^{\bar{B}X}$ $\hat{\pi}_{22}^{\bar{B}X}$ $\hat{\pi}_{13}^{\bar{B}X}$ $\hat{\pi}_{13}^{\bar{B}X}$

etc., (4 cards altogether)

Caution: the user must ensure that all start values here satisfy the condition that summing over the classes of a given manifest variable, with t fixed, yields a value of 1.0.

Example: For the above example, the start values might be the following, where columns correspond to the format.

Column:

1	9	17	25	33	41

1st card:

.8	.2	.7	.3	.6	.4

2nd card:

.7	.3	.4	.6	.5	.5

etc., (4 cards altogether).

10. Restrictions on the latent class probabilities (π_t^X)(optional*)   1–80 [20I2]   *Use only if columns 35–36 of Type 2 card is not blank. Enter 0 (or leave blank) the fields pertaining to *free* parameters. Enter 1 in fields pertaining to parameters which are *fixed*. (i.e., parameters constrained to be identical to

start values entered in card
Type 8 above.) Enter positive
integers greater than one in the
remaining fields: any two (or
more) integers equal to each other
will constrain those parameters to
be equal. The first field (columns
1–2) pertains to π_1^X; the
second field pertains to π_2^X;
etc.

Example: With a five-class model, where it is
desired to constrain the first latent class probability
to equal the start value, the second value is free, and
the next three values are constrained to equal each
other, enter the following numbers on the Type 10 card:

Column:
2 4 6 8 0
1 0 2 2 2

11. Restrictions on   1–80
the conditional   [2014]
probabilities
(optional*)

*Use only if columns 37–38
on Type 2 card are not
blank. Enter 0 (or leave
blank) in those fields pertaining
to *free* parameters. Enter 1
in those fields pertaining
to parameters constrained
to equal the start values
for that parameter. Enter
positive integers in the
remaining fields (integers
greater than 1): Any set of
integers equal to one another
will constrain the corresponding
parameters to be equal to each
other. Enter restrictions one

88

manifest variable at a time,
using, additional cards when
necessary. The correspondence
between fields of this card to
the conditional probabilities
is the same as that in the Type
9 card. *Within each latent class,
at least one parameter* **must** *be free
for each of the manifest variables,*
since one of the conditional
probability parameters within
each manifest variable, for each
latent class, is redundant.

Example: For the two-class model with dichotomous
manifest variables, the restrictions cards might look
the following.

Column:

  4 8 12 16

1st card:

  0 0 1 0   (i.e., $\pi_{11}^{\bar{A}X}, \pi_{21}^{\bar{A}X}$ are free: $\pi_{12}^{\bar{A}X}, \pi_{22}^{\bar{A}X}$ are fixed)

2nd card:

  2   2   (i.e., $\pi_{11}^{\bar{B}X} = \pi_{12}^{\bar{B}X}$ and $\pi_{21}^{\bar{B}X} = \pi_{22}^{\bar{B}X}$)

There must be as many restriction cards as
there are variables.

APPENDIX B

The MLLSA program lines listed below produced the results reported in Table 3.3. These lines represent the minimum set of commands for such an analysis. Only one of the available options (calculation of the χ^2 of the independence model) is requested. Appendix A provides a detailed description of each of the specific entries.

```
MODEL H2 (3 CLASS, UNRESTRICTED) RESPONDENT TYPE, 1982 GSS WHITES
 4 3  1202                    1
 2 3 3 2
(12F4.0)
 419 270  23  43  26  85  35  25   4   9   3  23
   2   4   1   2   0   6  71  42   6   9   1  13
  25  16   2   3   2  12   5   5   0   2   0   8
.56     .22     .22
.59     .41     .66     .34     .03     .97
.86     .07     .07     .85     .11     .04     .16     .39     .45
.95     .03     .02     .67     .29     .04     .60     .28     .12
.97     .03     .37     .63     .66     .34
```

The following program illustrates some of the options available with the MLLSA program—exact indicator and equality restrictions are specified for the conditional probabilities, and variable and value labels are specified for the observed measures. These commands provide the analysis for the data provided in Table 3.5.

```
MODEL H3.2 (3 CLASS, RESTRICTED) RESPONDENT TYPE, 1982 GSS WHITES
 4 3  1202                 1 1   1 1   1       1
 2 3 3 2
     ACUR    PURP    COOP    UNDR
     TRUE    NOT
     GOOD    DPND    WAST
     INTR    COOP    IMPH
     GOOD    FRPR
```

```
(12F4.0)
  419 270   23   43   26   85   35   25    4    9    3   23
    2   4    1    2    0    6   71   42    6    9    1   13
   25  16    2    3    2   12    5    5    0    2    0    8
 .56      .22      .22
 .62      .38      .62      .38      .00     1.0
 .86      .07      .07      .86      .07      .07      .16      .39      .45
 .95      .05      .00      .67      .29      .04      .60      .28      .12
1.0       .00      .37      .63      .66      .34
    2   0    2    0    1    0
    3   4    0    3    4    0    0    0    0
    0   0    1    0    0    0    0    0    0
    0   1    0    0    0    0
```

The MLLSA program lines listed below were used to constraint the conditional probabilities in the models reported in Chapter 4. Appendix A provides a detailed description of each of the specific entries.

MODEL H1 PROCTOR MODEL FOR 4 CAMPAIGN ITEMS 1980 ANES

```
    2   0    2    0    2    0    2    0    0    2
    2   0    2    0    2    0    0    2    0    2
    2   0    2    0    0    2    0    2    0    2
    2   0    0    2    0    2    0    2    0    2
```

MODEL H2 ITEM-SPECIFIC ERROR RATE MODEL FOR 4 CAMPAIGN ITEMS 1980 NES

```
    4   0    4    0    4    0    4    0    0    4
    5   0    5    0    5    0    0    5    0    5
    6   0    6    0    0    6    0    6    0    6
    7   0    0    7    0    7    0    7    0    7
```

H3 EQUAL TRUE-TYPE-SPECIFIC ERROR RATES MODEL 4 CAMPAIGN ITEMS 1980 NES

```
    2   0    3    0    4    0    5    0    0    6
    2   0    3    0    4    0    0    5    0    6
    2   0    3    0    0    4    0    5    0    6
    2   0    0    3    0    4    0    5    0    6
```

H4 LAZARSFELD'S LATENT-DISTANCE MODEL 4 CAMPAIGN ITEMS 1980 NES

```
    2   0    2    0    2    0    2    0    0    2
    3   0    3    0    3    0    0    4    0    4
    5   0    5    0    0    6    0    6    0    6
    7   0    0    7    0    7    0    7    0    7
```

H5 GOODMAN'S UNSCALABLE MODEL FOR 4 CAMPAIGN ITEMS 1980 NES

```
    1   0    1    0    1    0    1    0    0    1    0    0
    1   0    1    0    1    0    0    1    0    1    0    0
    1   0    1    0    0    1    0    1    0    1    0    0
    1   0    0    1    0    1    0    1    0    1    0    0
```

```
H6 GOODMAN'S UNSCALABLE MODEL FOR 4 CAMPAIGN ITEMS 1980 NES: BIFORM SCALE
    1   0   1   0   1   0   1   0   0   1   1   0   0   1   0   0
    1   0   1   0   1   0   0   1   0   1   1   0   1   0   0   0
    1   0   1   0   0   1   0   1   0   1   0   1   0   1   0   0
    1   0   0   1   0   1   0   1   0   1   1   0   0   1   0   0
H7 GOODMAN-PROCTOR UNSCALABLE MODEL 4 CAMPAIGN ITEMS 1980 NES
    2   0   2   0   2   0   2   0   0   2   0   0
    2   0   2   0   2   0   0   2   0   2   0   0
    2   0   2   0   0   2   0   2   0   2   0   0
    2   0   0   2   0   2   0   2   0   2   0   0
```

The MLLSA program lines listed below prodused the results reported in Chapter 5. The first set of program lines produced the results for the unrestricted, heterogeneous three-class model.

```
MODEL H1 (3 CLASS, UNRESTRICTED) 1982 GSS BLK AND WHT REPONDENT TYPE
 5 6  1649               1     1 1            1 2
 2 3 3 2 2
    ACUR    PURP    COOP    UNDR    RACE
    TRUE    NOT
    GOOD    DPND    WAST
    INTR    COOP    IMPH
    GOOD    FRPR
    WHTS    BLKS
(12F4.0)
 419 270   23   43   26   85   35   25    4    9    3   23
   2   4    1    2    0    6   71   42    6    9    1   13
  25  16    2    3    2   12    5    5    0    2    0    8
 117  95    7   19    6   30   14   10    1    1    0    9
   3   3    0    2    0    1   34   23    3    2    3    9
  19  14    1    1    1    7    5    2    0    1    0    4
.45      .15      .13      .13      .10      .04
.61      .39      .65      .35      .03      .97      .53      .47      .62      .38
.03      .97
.89      .05      .06      .91      .07      .02      .14      .23      .63      .87
.08      .05      .90      .05      .05      .08      .08      .74
.94      .05      .01      .69      .26      .05      .64      .26      .10      .97
.02      .01      .58      .35      .07      .64      .25      .11
.98      .02      .31      .69      .75      .25      .98      .02      .37      .63
.68      .32
1.0      .0      1.0      .0      1.0      .0      .0      1.0      .0      1.0
 .0     1.0
```

92

These MLLSA program lines produced the results reported in Table
5.4 for the unrestricted, partial homogeneity model for black and white
respondent types.

```
H10 RESTRICTED HOMOGENEITY MODEL: 1982 GSS WHITE AND BLACK RESPONDENT TYPES
 5 6  1649              1     1 1 1 1        1 2
 2 3 3 2 2
    ACUR    PURP    COOP    UNDR    RACE
    TRUE    NOT
    GOOD    DPND    WAST
    INTR    COOP    IMPH
    GOOD    FRPR
    WHTS    BLKS
(12F4.0)
 419 270  23  43  26  85  35  26   4   9   3  23
   2   4   1   2   0   6  71  42   6   9   1  13
  25  16   2   3   2  12   5   5   0   2   0   8
 117  95   7  19   6  30  14  10   1   1   0   9
   3   3   0   2   0   1  34  23   3   2   3   9
  19  14   1   1   1   7   5   2   0   1   0   4
.45     .15     .13     .13     .10     .04
.61     .39     .65     .35     .00     1.0     .53     .47     .62     .38
.0      1.0
.89     .05     .06     .91     .07     .02     .14     .23     .63     .87
.08     .05     .90     .05     .05     .08     .08     .74
.94     .06     .0      .69     .26     .05     .64     .26     .10     .97
.03     .0      .58     .35     .07     .64     .25     .11
1.0     .0      .31     .69     .75     .25     1.0     .0      .37     .63
.68     .32
1.0     .0      1.0     .0      1.0     .0      .0      1.0     .0      1.0
.0      1.0
 0 0 2 0 0 2
   7   0   7   0   1   0   7   0   7   0   1   0
   2   8   0   2   8   0   4  11   0   2   8   0   2   8   0   4  11   0
  15   0   1  14   0  10   5   6   0  15   0   1  14   0  10   5   6   0
   1   0  16   0  12   0   1   0  16   0  12   0
   0   0   0   0   0   0   0   0   0   0   0   0
```

REFERENCES

AITKIN, M., ANDERSON, D., and HINDE, J. (1981) "Statistical modelling of data on teaching styles," *Journal of the Royal Statistical Society*. Ser. A, **144**: 419–461.

ALDRICH, J. H. and NELSON, F. D. (1984) *Linear Probability, Logit, and Probit Models*. Sage University Papers: Quantitative Applications in the Social Science. Beverly Hills, CA: Sage.

ANDERSON, T. W. (1954) "On estimation of parameters in latent structure analysis," *Psychometrika* **19**: 1–10.

BERGAN, J. R. (1983) "Latent-class models in educational research." In W. E. Gordon (ed.) *Review of Research in Education*. Washington, D. C.: American Educational Research Association.

CLOGG, C. C. (1977) "Unrestricted and restricted maximum likelihood latent structure analysis: A manual for users." Working Paper 1977-09. University Park, PA: Population Issues Research Office.

———(1979) "Some latent structure models for the analysis of Likert-type data," *Social Science Research* **8**: 287–301.

———(1981a) "New developments in latent structure analysis." In D. M. Jackson and E. F. Borgatta (eds.) *Factor Analysis and Measurement* (pp. 215–246). Beverly Hills, CA: Sage.

———(1981b) "Latent structure models of mobility," *American Journal of Sociology* **86**: 836–868.

———(1984) "Some statistical models for analyzing why surveys disagree." In C. F. Turner and E. Martin (eds.) *Surveying Subjective Phenomena: Volume 2*. New York: Sage.

CLOGG, C. C. and GOODMAN, L. A. (1984) "Latent structure analysis of a set of multidimensional contingency tables," *Journal of the American Statistical Association* **79**: 762–771.

———(1985) "Simultaneous latent structure analysis in several groups." In N. B. Tuma (ed.) *Sociological Methodology*. San Fransisco: Josey-Bass.

———(1986) "On scaling models applied to data from several groups," *Psychometrika* **51**: 123–135.

94

CLOGG, C. C. and SAWYER, D. O. (1981) "A comparison of alternative models for analyzing the scalability of response patterns." In S. Leinhardt (ed.) *Sociological Methodology*. San Fransisco: Josey-Bass.

DAVIS, J. A. and SMITH, T. W. (1985) *General Social Surveys, 1972–1985*. [machine-readable data file]. Chicago: National Opinion Research Center.

DAYTON, C. M. and MACREADY, G. D. (1980) "A scaling model with response errors and intrinsically unscalable individuals," *Psychometrika* **45**: 343–356.

DILLON, W. R. and GOLDSTEIN, M. (1984) *Multivariate Analysis: Methods and Applications*. New York: Wiley.

DEMPSTER, A. P., LAIRD, N. M., and RUBIN, D. B. (1977) "Maximum likelihood from incomplete data via the EM algorithm (with discussion)," *Journal of the Royal Statistical Society*, series B **39**: 1-38.

GOODMAN, L. A. (1972) "A general model for the analysis of surveys," *American Journal of Sociology* **77**: 1035–1086.

———(1974a) "Exploratory latent structure analysis using both identifiable and unidentifiable models," *Biometrika* **61**: 215–231.

———(1974b) "The analysis of systems of qualitative variables when some of the variables are unobservable. Part I-A: Modified latent structure approach," *American Journal of Sociology* **79**: 1179–1259.

———(1975) "A new model for scaling response patterns: An application of the quasi-independence concept," *Journal of the American Statistical Association* **70**: 755–768.

———(1979) "On the estimation of parameters in latent structure analysis," *Psychometrika* **44**: 123–128.

GOODMAN, L. A. and KRUSKAL, W. H. (1954) "Measures of association for cross-classification," *Journal of the American Statistical Association* **49**: 732–764.

GREEN, B. F. (1951) "A general solution for the latent class model of latent structure analysis," *Psychometrika* **16**: 151–166.

———(1952) "Latent structure analysis and its relation to factor analysis," *Journal of the American Statistical Association* **47**: 71-76.

HABERMAN, S. J. (1974) "Log-linear models for frequency tables derived by indirect observation: Maximum likelihood equations," *Annals of Statistics* **2**: 911-924.

———(1979) *Analysis of Qualitative Data. Vol. 2: New Developments*. New York: Academic Press.

HENRY, N. W. (1983) "Latent structure analysis." in S. Kotz and N. L. Johnson (eds.) *Encyclopedia of Statistical Sciences* (pp. 497–504). New York: Wiley.

JÖRESKOG, K. G. and SÖRBOM, D. (1979) *Advances in Factor Analysis and Structural Equation Models.* Cambridge, MA: Abt Books.

LAZARSFELD, P. F. (1950a) "The logical and mathematical foundations of latent structure analysis." In S. A. Stouffer et al. (eds.) *Measurement and Prediction.* Princeton, NJ: Princeton University Press.

———(1950b) "The interpretation and computation of some latent structures." In S. A. Stouffer et al. (eds.) *Measurement and Prediction.* Princeton, NJ: Princeton University Press.

LAZARSFELD, P. F. and HENRY, N. W. (1968) *Latent Structure Analysis.* Boston: Houghton Mifflin.

MADDALA, G. S. (1983) *Limited-Dependent and Qualitative Variables in Econometrics.* Cambridge: Cambridge University Press.

MADDEN, T. J. and DILLON, W. R. (1982) "Causal analysis and latent class models: An application to a communication hierarchy of effects model," *Journal of Marketing Research* 19: 472–490.

MANDANSKY, A. (1968) "Latent structure." In D. L.Sills (ed.) *International Encyclopedia of the Social Sciences* (pp. 33–38). New York: Macmillan Free Press.

MARSDEN, P. (1985) "Latent structure models for relationally defined social classes," *American Journal of Sociology* 90: 1002–1021.

MCCUTCHEON, A. L. (1985) "A latent class analysis of tolerance for nonconformity in the American public," *Public Opinion Quarterly* 49: 474–488.

———(1986) "Sexual morality, pro-life values, and attitudes toward abortion: A simultaneous latent structure analysis for 1978-83." Paper presented at the Annual Meeting of the Eastern Sociological Society, New York, NY, April, 1986.

MCHUGH, R. B. (1956) "Efficient estimation and local identification in latent class analysis," *Psychometrika* 21: 331–347.

MILLER, W. E. (1982) *American National Election Study, 1980.* [machine readable data file]. Ann Arbor, MI: Inter-university Consortium for Political and Social Research.

MOOIJAART, A. (1982) "Latent structure analysis for categorical variables." In K. G. Jöreskog and H. Wold *Systems Under Indirect Observation.* Amsterdam: North-Holland.

96

PROCTOR, C. H. (1970) "A probabilistic formulation and statistical analysis of Guttman scaling," *Psychometrika* 35: 73–78.

RINDSKOPF, D. and RINDSKOPF, W. (1986) "The value of latent class analysis in medical diagnosis," *Statistics in Medicine* 5: 21–27.

ROSENBERG, M. (1968) *The Logic of Survey Analysis*. New York: Basic Books.

SROLE, L. (1956) "Social integration and certain corollaries," *American Sociological Review* 21: 709–716.

STINCHCOMBE, A. L. (1968) *Constructing Social Theories*. New York: Harcourt-Brace.

STOUFFER, S. A. and TOBY, J. (1951) "Role conflict and personality," *American Journal of Sociology* 56: 395–406.

TAYLOR, D. G. (1983) "Analyzing qualitative data." In P. H. ROSSI, J. D. WRIGHT, and A. B. ANDERSON, (eds.) *Handbook of Survey Research*. Orlando: Academic.

TAYLOR, M. C. (1983) "The black-and-white model of attitude stability: A latent class examination of opinion and nonopinion in the American public," *American Journal of Sociology* 89: 373–401.

TORGERSON, W. S. (1962) *Theory and Methods of Scaling*. New York: Wiley.

TUCH, S. A. (1981) "Analyzing recent trends in prejudice toward blacks: Insights from latent class models," *American Journal of Sociology* 87: 130–142.

YOUNG, M. A. (1983) "Evaluating diagnostic criteria: A latent class paradigm," *Journal of Psychiatric Research* 17: 285–296.

YOUNG, M. A., TANNER, M. A., and MELTZER, H. Y. (1982) "Operational definitions of schizophrenia: What do they identify?" *Journal of Nervous and Mental Disease* 170: 443–447.

ABOUT THE AUTHOR

ALLAN L. MCCUTCHEON is assistant professor of Sociology at the University of Delaware, where he teaches political sociology and quantitative methods. He holds a Ph.D. from the University of Chicago and has authored and co-authored papers on political, religious, and social attitudes and behavior as well as on methods. His primary research interest is the modeling of sociopolitical attitudes and behavior.